THE AMERICAN FAMILY

Volume 70, Sage Library of Social Research

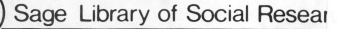

Sage Library of Social Resear

The American Family

A Demographic History

Rudy Ray Seward

Foreword by HERMAN R. LANTZ

Volume 70
SAGE LIBRARY OF
SOCIAL RESEARCH

 SAGE PUBLICATIONS   Beverly Hills   London

For information address:

SAGE PUBLICATIONS, INC.
275 South Beverly Drive
Beverly Hills, California 90212

SAGE PUBLICATIONS LTD
28 Banner Street
London EC1Y 8QE

Printed in the United States of America

Library of Congress Cataloging in Publication Data

Seward, Rudy Ray.
    The American family.

    (Sage library of social research ; v. 70)
    Bibliography: p.
    1. Family—United States—History. 2. Family
research—United States. 3. Urbanization—United
States. 4. Industrialization. I. Title.
HQ535.S44   301.42'0973   78-19609
ISBN 0-8039-1112-2
ISBN 0-8039-1113-0 pbk.

SECOND PRINTING

CONTENTS

FOREWORD

The interest in family history as an intellectual endeavor has its origins in the nineteenth century. In that period such interest was part of a larger preoccupation with social evolution. Scholars searched for family origins and speculated about the evolution of different kinds of family structures. Underlying much of this search were certain value-laden assumptions regarding the place of the traditional, white, western, patriarchal family in relation to family structures elsewhere. And these values became the basis of judgment in assessing family structures in time and space. This orientation continued into the twentieth century, but in America the writings took another form. While speculation about the family in the past remained, there were efforts to introduce occasional primary source materials as a basis for family history. Thus in the writings of George Howard and Arthur Calhoun, for example, one finds some use of court records, diaries, and selected public documents. Yet even these writings were clouded by certain biases regarding the nature of the early American family. Writers saw this family as large, patriarchal, integrated, stable, and organized around the economic concerns of its members. There was little recognition of the existence of family patterns that were at variance with these views. Writers failed to appreciate the extent of female power, the existence of romantic love, and the extent of marital incompatibility that existed. The conceptual trap that characterized many who wrote about the family is to be found in their particular formulation of family change. While it would be incorrect to assume that all writers shared the same views, many

have shared a common notion regarding the role of urbanization and industrialization as the major variables in family
change. And in many respects they shared an overly simplified
view of the role of each. Not possessing the necessary, accurate
information about the past, they have found it easy to see the
modern family as a very different family. Just as evolutionary
doctrine dominated the perspective of scholars in the last century, so has the uncritical acceptance of urbanization and industrialization dominated the thinking of scholars in the twentieth century. It is understandable that this has been the case.
The products of modernization were everywhere to be seen.
The concentration of people, both in the cities and in the factory, brought to the forefront the problems of social transformation in ways that were dramatic. There were social problems of the family, single people without roots, families living
in crowded space, deviance, individualism, and marital incompatibility. These were seen as new difficulties not experienced
in the past. The use of urbanization and industrialization as
explanatory variables for family change was viewed in its
broadest sense, without regard to such basic problems as the
relationship of these variables to one another, that is, separating out those influences due to urbanization from those due to
industrialization, the matter of ideological variables in relation to other variables, and the very complex question of how
and under what circumstances each becomes a change agent.

Within the last decade there has been an upsurge of new
social history which has addressed itself to the family. This
family history differs from older family history in three respects. First, the history is based on the empirical reconstruction of the family. There are innovative techniques across a
broad spectrum of data ranging from the systematic examination of public records to the examination of literary sources,
including magazines and books. Second, there have been efforts to establish base lines in terms of what the family was
like at a given point in time. The importance of base lines is
that they make it possible to examine and measure family
change from one period to another. If scholars had addressed

this question during an earlier period, we would have been on much firmer ground in the assertions made about the early American family. Third, the new family history gives promise of providing further insights into a broad theoretical issue that would delineate both the important macroscopic changes and how such changes are reflected in family change.

The reexamination of the relationship of modernization to family change remains an important research objective, and such research is starting to take on new dimensions in academic departments both in this country and abroad. At Southern Illinois University several projects are underway. Professor Lewellyn Hendrix is extending such an analysis to the field of music as a source of data. He has completed a content analysis of folk music in this country and in Europe in order to determine the kinds of concerns expressed toward love, sex, and marriage during the preindustrial and industrial periods. His study provides us both with new information and a new data source for the understanding of the family. John Murphy is studying the perceptions of the aged in America during both the preindustrial and industrial periods. His work will demonstrate that the negative image of the aged, along with the social problems of the aged, existed before industrialization. Martin Schultz is studying divorce rates in the period prior to the collection of federal statistics. His work will shed light on the nature and extent of marital incompatibility in the preindustrial period.

In spite of the promise of such developments, problems with new family history remain. From a professional viewpoint the documentation of any set of family patterns in the past is important because such work provides us with a recording of the past, yet there is the danger that some of this work will lead to a preoccupation with the unique and unusual, a problem which has characterized traditional historical work. There is already an indication of writings which reflect basically antiquarian interests that are likely to be of limited value for those who wish to understand the family. When the study of a single family system is dealt with in a way that enables us to under-

stand how family organization bears a relationship to historical
forces, we will begin to understand both historical and social
dynamics better than we now do, and we shall be able to understand how family patterns are shaped by a socio-historic
milieu. In this quest we shall have to guard against any premature closing off of new sources of data because of their
qualitative nature, or because the data themselves are not
amenable to conventional methodological techniques. This
may mean that the single investigator may have to stake out
and exploit new data sources when the field of the family may
not yet be ready to accept these.

The book prepared by Rudy Seward is an important illustra-
tion of how much the new family history can accomplish. Rudy
Seward has reexamined the validity of long-held beliefs regarding the composition of the early American family. In so doing
he has raised an important theoretical question regarding the
relationship of family structure to broad modernization variables. Seward's work is important for several reasons. First, it
exemplifies how an innovative examination of data available for
a long time enables us to reformulate our understanding of
family structure. Second, this study establishes base lines for
the structure of the American family in the past. Seward shows
that the nuclear family in America has always been and continues to be the predominant type. Moreover, the typical
American family was small, mobile, and independent. Third,
this study raises important questions about the facile use which
has been made of modernization variables to explain changes in
the family. Seward reports, for example, that extended families
were on the increase in America in the 1850-1880 period, a
time of intensive industrialization. In a direct test of the response of families to industrial and nonindustrial environments,
Seward finds the amount of variance explained by industrial-
urban factors to be low to nonexistent. He concludes that the
family has maintained a high level of structural integrity, and
that the role of external pressures has been minimal. These
findings clearly indicate that we shall have to pay much more
attention to the complex relationship involved in understanding

how such features of modernization as industrialization have resulted in family change. The notion that the typical American family in the past was large and then became significantly smaller as a result of industrialization has been found in virtually every book that has dealt with the family, and such views have found their way into lectures for college students for many decades. This effort by Seward goes a long way toward undoing some of the misconceptions regarding the early American family. His work is also a reminder that our knowledge of institutions like the family needs periodic reexamination. It is not only necessary to assume that our knowledge of the family is tentative, it is also necessary to assume that much of it may be false. Rudy Seward addresses this matter in the study before us. For this he deserves our appreciation and gratitude.

Herman R. Lantz
Southern Illinois University

AUTHOR'S PREFACE

Almost a decade ago, I became intrigued by the topic and study of family history. As this interest was nurtured through readings, it soon became apparent that more was known historically about the ideal than the real patterns of the American family. A common but untested contention in many of these descriptions, and for that matter family literature in general, was the role that the processes of industrialization and urbanization had played in bringing about dramatic changes in the family over time.

Several scholars, including William J. Goode and Herman R. Lantz, insightfully diagnosed the limitations of existing knowledge in family history and delineated the major directions for future research, which included the following: document real family patterns in the past; establish historical baselines to measure the extent of change; and determine the influence of industrialization and urbanization. These three general concerns became the basis for my research interest. Data sources were not readily available, but the family statistics reported by the United States' Bureau of the Census appeared to be a potentially valuable source for historical data if attention was limited to family structure. Closer examination revealed that comparable data on family characteristics were available only going back several decades. The census has only consistently presented family size since 1790, but even this was inadequate because prior to 1930 no distinction was made between household and family units. Next I learned that the original manuscript census schedules were available, and an exploratory study using a sample of 1850 schedules demonstrated that sufficient information was available to establish real patterns, baselines, and the amount of change for many different aspects of the American family. This use of the schedules was limited to the last half of the nineteenth century, but fortunately some comparable data for the American colonial period became available from the research by demographic historians. Together these data sources do provide a historical description and comparison of the American family structure.

Thinking back over this project's development, I am reminded of the many people who unselfishly contributed their time and energy. My greatest debt is to Herman R. Lantz, who by way of his works and instruction generated an interest in the problem, helped in a realistic definition of the project, and constantly provided encouraging and stimulating commentary. For valuable assistance at different stages of the project I am indebted to: Jerry Gaston, Lewellyn Hendrix, and Gunnar Boalt. Grants from the National Science Foundation, the Department of Sociology at Southern Illinois University, and the Faculty Research Program at North Texas State University supported in part the collection, analysis, and interpretation of the data. Valuable editorial and secretarial skills were donated by Peggy Miller, Rosie Kimble, and Martha Casey. Finally, I am indebted to both my wife, Jean, and my son, Rudy Allyn, who provided both assistance and necessary encouragement by adding a dimension to life that made it all seem worthwhile. To all of these people and others too numerous to mention I will be forever grateful.

Chapter 1

INTRODUCTION

The family, all observers would surely agree, has undergone many and various transformations throughout the history of mankind, although few if any would fully agree upon either an explanation of this change or the course it has taken. Limiting our attention to the last two centuries, however, there does appear to be consensus about the direction and the causes of family change: namely, that the family has changed from a large, influential, extended unit to a small, mobile, independent unit as a result of the development and growth of industrialization and urbanization. Within societies, extended families should be more predominant in rural areas than in urban areas. Cross-culturally, extended families should be more predominant in underdeveloped countries. Historically then, as a society becomes more industrialized and urbanized, extended families will decline and be replaced by the smaller nuclear family unit.

Focus of the Study

The questions raised in this study are as follows:

(1) Has the American family made such a transition from a prevalence of extended families to a prevalence of nuclear families? Data on certain structural aspects of the family unit from the colonial period to the present time provide the basis for this analysis.

(2) What effect, if any, has the processes of industrialization and urbanization had upon family units?

The generalized relationship of the family to the processes of industrialization and urbanization is usually started in such a general and ambiguous manner that it is impossible to empirically prove or disprove. Consequently, to aid in achieving the two objectives of this study several concerns must be dealt with. These concerns, when addressed, will allow us a more accurate description of family structure and will test the impact of industrialization and urbanization on the family:

(1) The definition of the family concept utilized by this study. What determines the boundaries of the family has often varied. Blood ties, legal ties, place of residence, social interaction, or physical interaction—each of these, and various combinations, have been used to determine the boundaries of the family unit, but there is no clear consensus as to which is the most accurate or appropriate.

(2) A distinction between ideal and real family patterns and whether change is occurring for only one of these patterns or both. This is an important differentiation because the majority of families in some societies do not or cannot exhibit the expected ideal patterns.

(3) A definition and description of the industrialization process. Much of the work that cites industrialization as a prime independent force in changing the family fails to delineate what the process entails and to attempt to measure the effects of industrialization upon the family. The development of the industrialization process will be described, and several available

indices of its development will be used as industrialization variables. These variables will then be used to test the effects, if any, of this process upon the family.

(4) The urbanization process will also be assessed. A number of available characteristics of urbanization will be measured and their relationship to the family will be explored.

(5) Finally, the family's role in limiting or facilitating industrialization will be explored. Only recently has there been an emphasis in family literature upon the family's role in the development of the processes industrialization and urbanization.

These then are the objectives and concerns of this study. To meet these a wide variety of sources and data will be used.

The first objective, a historical description, and the first two concerns will be dealt with by utilizing data covering the entire development of the American family—from the colonial period to the present. The colonial data will be presented in Chapter 2. The descriptive data on the colonial family are derived primarily from recent work done in demographic history. As a result of this work, available family structural data on the colonial American family can be compared to more recent data. The next period for which structural data on the family are presented is the latter half of the nineteenth century. These data are presented in Chapter 3. With the availability of the manuscript census schedules, it was possible to provide a thorough description of family structure during this period. A grant from the National Science Foundation (GS-33863) made possible collection of a large, national, and representative sample of families upon which to base this description. Finally, family data for this century that are comparable to the earlier data are presented in Chapter 5. These contemporary data were taken from the published Bureau of the Census reports. Hence, it is possible to present some comparable family structural data for various time periods over the last four centuries that provide a basis for observing what changes have taken place historically.

The second objective and the final three concerns of the study are dealt with in Chapter 4. In this chapter the development of industrialization and, to a lesser extent, urbanization are outlined from their beginnings in the United States. How the structure of the American family has varied during the different stages of the development of these processes is also described. However, a more direct test of the effects of industrialization and urbanization upon the family is made possible by using the sample families collected from the manuscript census schedules for the last half of the nineteenth century. It is possible for each sample family to be linked to different values on several industrialization and urbanization variables. Through statistical analysis it is possible to identify any association between these two processes, as measured by these variables, and family structure. This analysis becomes even more significant in light of the fact that this period was a time of intense industrialization and urbanization in the United States. These latter data and their analysis provide some of the specifics of historical, societal change. At this point little is known beyond the general trends about societal change. This study will attempt to elucidate some of the complicated relationships that may have existed between the family and other social systems and processes.

This investigation, apart from its specific focus, may provide a better understanding of societal change in general. In particular, it may well lead to a clearer understanding of the role of industrialization and urbanization, cited by many as the primary independent variables, in societal change over the last two centuries. In addition, this should give us a better understanding of the relationship between various structures in society.

The Study of the American Family: A Changing Perspective

There is widespread support for the belief that the American family has gone through several important and drastic changes over time. Most of these arguments focus upon the processes of industrialization and urbanization as the major causes of these changes.

The family unit that existed prior to the effects of these two processes is usually characterized as large, extended, influential, and stable. The large size of the family was attributed to the fact that many adult kinfolk and a large number of children all shared the same housing unit. The family was influential in that it had primary responsibility and control over a wide range of its members' activities. Hence, throughout an individual's life, most of the social roles he performed were under the direct or indirect control of his family. This influence can be summarized by listing the functions for which the family was primarily responsible, such as procreation, socialization, education, economic support, protection, religion, and recreation. The family was thought to be fairly self-sufficient as an economic unit. It had to produce most of the goods and services that were necessary for its survival. Because survival was often a difficult task, it was necessary that every member work toward it. Each member had to be assigned specific tasks and had to perform them conscientiously.

Family members were very dependent upon one another and were expected to deemphasize individual interests in favor of family interests as a whole. As a result, this type of family unit has been considered a very stable one. Even when children had grown and were ready for marriage, their parents had considerable control over their mate selection. After marriage, the couple usually resided with or near the bridegroom's parents. The fact that few marriages were dissolved through divorce contributed significantly to an image of family stability. These are some of the major characteristics of the type of family unit that presumedly preceded the development of industrialization and urbanization.

FAMILY CHANGE: THE TRADITIONAL PERSPECTIVE

Numerous and various sources have provided support for this image of the preindustrial family. Many do not explicitly describe but implicitly suggest a preindustrial family unit when they discuss the changes in the family that resulted from the impact of industrialization and urbanization.

Popular literature is full of commentary about the declining size, importance, and stability that is a part of the contemporary American family. It is alleged that the demands of a modern industrialized society produce structural changes in the family unit making it less stable. Articles devote much space to detailing the chaos, confusion, destruction, and structural changes occurring in the contemporary family (cf., Hunt, 1971: 116-118, 168-175). Also, until very recently most introductory sociology textbooks presented similar arguments, placing an emphasis upon several structural and functional changes in the family brought about by the processes of industrialization and urbanization (cf., Horton and Hunt, 1968: 232; McKee, 1969:365).

Works devoted exclusively to family material also give much support to the traditional perspective of family change. Calhoun (1919), in his frequently cited work on the American family, presented the stereotypic view of the family as changing from a large extended unit to a smaller nuclear one. In the colonial period marriage occurred at a very young age (p. 67), the unmarried were distrusted, the rapid remarriage of widows was common, and families were very large (p. 87). Calhoun portrayed the family as the cornerstone of colonial life. Emphasizing the effect of the "movement of political democracy," Calhoun (p. 169) noted that the family unit had gone from a "collectivity of blood relatives of several generations under a ruling head" to "the establishment of entirely independent families built around the personal independence of the young husband and his relation to his wife."

Burgess, Locke, and Thomes (1963:335), with much the same perspective as Calhoun, noted the existence "a hundred years ago in the United States [of] a stable network of familial expectations, roles, and values . . . which controlled and circumscribed the behavior to the individual families." As a result of the transformation to an "urban, industrial culture," there had been a number of "radical modifications" in family patterns. Goode (1963:6) claimed that as "the economic system expands through industrialization, family patterns change. Extended kinship ties weaken . . . [and] some form of the conjugal system generally begin to appear."

A great deal of agreement exists concerning the type of alleged changes in the family. The focus is usually on how the family has changed both structurally and functionally. In most cases both structural and functional change are dealt with by the observer, but many times one type of change or only several aspects of change are emphasized. Among the more important (and most frequently mentioned) structural changes resulting from the processes of industrialization and urbanization are a decline in family size, a weakening of kinship ties, a decline in the association of generations, a decreasing of birth rate, a rising divorce rate, and a change in family role definitions. Some of the more important functional changes include a decline in the control of the family over many of its historic functions, such as the economic, protective, educational, recreational, and religious functions (cf., Burgess and Locke, 1953; Ogburn, 1969:58-63; Ogburn and Nimkoff, 1955:99-100). An important part of the general argument is the stress upon the compatibility of the nuclear family unit with "modern" society. Kephart (1961:73) predicted that "if the trend toward urbanism, industrialism, and mobility spreads to other parts of the world, it is just possible that the consanquine [extended] type of family organization will tend to disappear." Parsons (1964:177-198) described the resulting contemporary family as a more specialized and dependent unit which has become structurally isolated.

In most of these works the process of industrialization is emphasized more than that of urbanization. It is frequently taken for granted that the two processes have developed concomitantly, but industrialization is sometimes considered the independent variable. It is conventionally argued that various aspects of industrialization brought about the concentration and congestion of a once dispersed, rural population in the United States. The availability of jobs in industry resulted in migration from the farms and small towns. As Martinson (1970:76) described it, "Industry was the new frontier." However, the promise and necessity of the new frontier was rooted in an excess labor supply as a result of an agricultural system that was becoming rapidly mechanized. He stressed that the industrialization process was "the major economic force responsible for the modern American family" (p. 75). Nimkoff (1965:61-62) also identified industrialization as the "independent variable" and the family unit as the "dependent variable" in the change relationships.

Another common theme is noted in Nimkoff's assertion that the family is the "dependent variable." This theme emphasizes the family's role as a passive agent in social change. Martinson (1970:375) provided an example of this theme when he stated that the "family is not a dominant social system in initiating social change." Although the family can be selective in its adaptations, "to a greater extent than other major social systems, [it] facilitates social change by adapting" (pp. 375-376).

Although less emphasized, the effects of urbanization upon the family have also been described. Wirth (1938) provided on of the earlier and most detailed descriptions of the effects of urbanization upon the family unit. In "relatively large, dense, and permanent settlements of socially heterogenous individuals" (p. 8) there is a decrease of intimate personal relationships and an increase in the segmentalization of human relations. Although physical contacts are close, social contacts become distant or as Wirth describes them "anonymous, superficial and transitory" (p. 1).

Urban life was seen by Wirth (pp. 20-24) as bringing about a decline in the social importance of the family and the breakdown or weakening of kinship bonds. Families in urban areas are smaller and often have no children. The family unit socially has been freed from the larger kinship structure which is an important characteristic of rural life. Individual family members pursue their own diverging interests in different institutional structures of the community. In urban communities many organizations have taken over functions or responsibilities once handled by the family, e.g., maintenance of health, cultural advancement, and recreation.

Nimkoff (1947), like many other writers of his period, presented what appears to be a biased view that favored the rural extended type of family. Urban areas were cited as unfavorable and unfit environments for the rearing of children while rural areas, which provide plenty of space and freedom for the child, were seen as possessing the necessary conditions for the healthy development of the young. In urban areas the activities were generally more individualistic than in rural areas where the family often acted as one unit (p. 143-145).

Burgess and Locke (1953) also described the disintegration of the extended rural family in urban areas. They saw these changes as undermining and transforming a "social order [that was] essentially rural in its nature" (Burgess and Locke, 1953: 120-121). In the rural areas the family was of uppermost importance. Its role was tightly defined by norms and enforced by pressures of intimate and face-to-face contacts. The norms and pressures that regulated the rural family were broken down in urban areas. As a result of the decline in the institutional functions performed by the family, the stability of the family has become more dependent upon the affection and congeniality of its members and less dependent upon the conceptions evident in the "extended family." The family, therefore, was no longer seen as an important institutional structure in the urban area.

In addition to these structural and functional family changes, a change in certain values is reported to have taken place that affected the family. Lantz and Snyder (1969:48-49) emphasized a number of ideas and doctrines which contributed to these value changes. These were the doctrines of secularism, humanism, and democracy. Secularism made man more confident of his ability to create and modify the customs, traditions, and standards of behavior that compose his culture. Previously "fixed" societal standards become subject of man's continual reexamination and challenge. Humanism reinforced secularism by legitimatizing a belief in the individualistic worth of the human personality. This belief contributed to a growing trust in man's ability to determine the societal standards constituting his culture. Finally, democracy supported every individual's right to participate in the determination of his own situation and societal standards. These ideological doctrines and the values associated with them have provided modern man with the intellectual equipment to undertake a more active role in shaping his life situation. The new concept of man's role in the determination of his own life situation contributed to changes in the family system. Unlike the situation in the past, changes in the family system were determined more by the members of the family unit rather than by external forces, such as demographic, economic, social, and religious pressures.

The direction of these self-determined changes were gradually manifested by a shift in family goals. The new goals included a concern for the comfort and welfare of each and every family unit member and led to considerations limiting the contemporary family to a smaller nuclear unit (cf., Lantz and Snyder, 1969:69; Levy, 1965:57). First, with a major reduction of infant mortality and a greater probability that each child will survive, maximum fertility is no longer necessary to assure posterity and an abundant supply of members to fill the positions necessary for family survival. Second, children are no longer an economic necessity for helping to provide for the family but are instead additional units of consumption which have to be fed, clothed, and socialized. Third, to maintain economic security and provide greater material advantages for a child, a smaller number of children in the family unit is necessary. A smaller family unit can also increase the chances for social mobility for both the parents and the children. Another consideration is that large families today are often perceived as being associated with a lower socio-economic position; and family size is consequently held down. Finally, limiting the number of children can also be seen as resulting from parents' decision to follow their own interests rather than devoting most of their lives to the rearing of children. These considerations reflect, then, the new values and goals held by the contemporary family and the effect they have had upon family change.

In surveying the literature concerning the treatment of family change from a traditional perspective, it becomes apparent that much "contamination" exists among these various works. They often quote one another as sources, and a number of initial sources are either directly or indirectly used by almost all the works. A primary reason for this situation is the condition of the data themselves. Data on the family before the turn of the century have been extremely limited. Letters, diaries, and personal papers provided the basis for almost all of the family history before 1900. Calhoun's (1919) history of the American family is based almost exclusively on such sources. The Calhoun work is an example of one "key" source that has been heavily relied upon in the past and in the present (cf., Edwards, 1969:12). Of related interest is the evaluation by historians of the study of the American family. Demos (1968:40) characterized the area of American family history as an aspect of American history which has been "badly served by unsystematic, impressionistic methods of handling source materials." Bailyn, in 1966, commenting on the state of most family studies, observed that it was possible "to prove any reasonable theory about the family" (Saveth, 1969: 317). Sociologists have also observed the dismal state of family studies (cf., Goode, 1963:1-23; Lantz et al., 1968:413-426). The prime concern for sociologists lies with the almost nonexistent documentation of "baselines" for the American family (Lantz et al., 1968:425). Because the majority of the data about the early American family are impressionistic, it has seemed virtually impossible to measure what change or changes, if any, have taken place. Historical documentation of the American family's characteristics would provide "baselines" to measure change. Thus sociologists and historians agree that a need exists for detailed and precise information in the family area.

CHALLENGES TO THE TRADITIONAL PERSPECTIVE

Although we have been considering what can be safely termed the common perspective of family change that has occurred historically, numerous works have not shared this perspective. There are at least four different approaches: definitional indistinctions, structural exceptions, behavioral pattern exceptions, and external limitations.

Definitional indistinctions refer to those challenges of the initial generalization that are based upon its implications for family unit boundaries. There are two different directions this type of challenge has taken. One points to the cross-cultural importance and viability of the nuclear family throughout history. As Murdock (1949:7) pointed out, the nuclear family has, in all societies surveyed, "existed as a distinct and strongly functional group." Spiro (1954:839-846) also noted that the roles of the nuclear family are universal although they do not always form a recognized unit.

The other direction of this type of challenge was stimulated by Parsons' discussion of the "isolation of the nuclear family" (Parsons and Bales, 1955:9-11). These challenges documented the extent and significance of kinship relations in urban and industrial areas and showed the viability of the extended family. Many of the studies that took this stance supported the conclusions of Sussman and Burchinal (1964:170-176) who found "numerous behavioral exchanges involving aid, social interaction, and services extended taking place within the kin group." They concluded that the contemporary family unit was a "modified" extended system and not an independent, "isolated" nuclear system as had been suggested (cf., Dotson, 1951; Axelrod, 1956; Sussman, 1959; Litwak, 1960).

Although much was written concerning this issue, the issue was to a large extent, contrived. As Parsons (1965:34) stated these "two views are not contradictory but complementary." Parsons was not saying that all relationships with outside kin are broken, but merely that the extended kinship relations which do exist "do not form firmly structured units of the social system." If nothing else these studies do emphasize the need for an explicit definition of family unit boundaries.

The second group of challengers provide structural exceptions to expected family structures as they are stated in the initial generalization. For example, Greenfield (1961:312-322) noted the existence of the extended family in industrialized Japan and of the nuclear family on the agricultural island of Barbados. He also pointed to the existence of the nuclear family in seventeenth century England prior to its industrialization and colonization of America. Work in the area of historical demography also supports and elaborates upon Greenfield's point. For example, P. Laslett (1965b:89-94) challenged a number of common myths about preindustrial England. He indicated that the typical family in the rural communities of England was, in fact, nuclear in structure, and he presented evidence that families were smaller in size in preindustrial society than previously believed. P. Laslett (1970:75-87) and E. A. Wrigley were founding members of the Cambridge Group for the History of Population and Social Structure at Cambridge University. Its primary objective was to explore the size and structure of households and families over the last five hundred years in England and other countries (France, Serbia, Japan, other areas of Western Europe, and colonial North America). Although the mean size of households varied, no evidence was found to suggest that the extended family predominated in any of these locations over the period studied (P. Laslett and Wall, 1972).

Support for structural exceptions in the American family has also been presented. A number of historians have recently presented data suggesting that the nuclear family was the dominant type during the American colonial period. (A detailed discussion of these data is presented in the next chapter.) In addition, evidence is available suggesting the lack of extended family structures in the nineteenth century American family (Seward, 1974). Cross-cultural evidence also exists concerning the lack of extended family structures throughout a period of industrial development for a given nation (c.f., Orenstein, 1961).

The third approach demonstrates the existence of behavioral patterns that deviate from the initial expectations derived from the generalization. Lantz et al. (1968:413-426; 1973:566-588) provided evidence suggesting the existence of behavior patterns in colonial America widely presumed to be a result of industrialization. In a content analysis of colonial magazines, they found the existence of the "romantic love complex" in the mate selection process. Although some discussions in the colonial magazines supported the traditional view of emphasizing economic goals and parental control in mate selection, the majority of discussions involved the element of romantic love. Emphasis was placed upon "personal happiness" in mate choice. The data on the authority pattern in the family supported the prevalence of male authority, but, at the same time, some emphasis was placed upon "subtle female power." The data suggested that male authority was often mediated by certain forms of female power. Furstenburg (1966:326-327) in his content analysis of diaries written by European travelers visiting the United States during the first half of the nineteenth century found that an emphasis upon romantic love existed during this period and, in fact, the process of mate selection was very similar to the process today (pp.329-331). His evidence also challenged the idea that family cohesion was much stronger during this earlier period. Furstenburg (p. 337) suggested that some of the strains that led to reduced cohesion may in fact have "eased the adaptation to an industrial society," not the reverse. Recent works by Smith (1973a; 1973b) have suggested that the breakdown of extended family cohesion, "intergenerational control," occurred during the preindustrial period of the middle and late eighteenth century. Using a sample of "reconstituted" family units from Hingham, Massachusetts, Smith found a declining influence of parents over the marriage (age, order, and chances), migration, and premarital sexual behavior of their offspring. Hence growing evidence suggests that changes in behavioral patterns occurred before the process of industrialization and urbanization developed.

The final approach in challenging the generalized relationship argues that external forces limited the formation of the family structure, regardless of the ideal expectations. This approach emphasizes economic and/or demographic limitations. Sjoberg (1960:157-163) argued that in preindustrial societies only upper-class urban dwellers could afford to maintain the extended family pattern. The majority of the lower-class population in urban and rural areas could not exhibit the extended family pattern even if they were inclined to do so. The Hsu (1943), Lang (1946), and Levy (1949) studies of the Chinese family argued that economic limitations, among other factors, limited to the wealthy upper class the attainment of an extended family structure. Collver (1963) emphasized the role of demographic factors in circumscribing the family structure in India. Theoretical efforts by Goode (1963) and Levy (1965:40-63) developed the arguments of these earlier works and expanded them to encompass most of the societies of the world. Levy's argument was stated in such a general manner as to include all societies past, present, and future, and in propositional form with the explicit hope that it would lend itself to empirical verification. Levy (1965:41) summarized his view as follows: "The general outlines and nature of the actual family structures have been virtually identical in certain strategic respects in all known societies in world history for well over 50 percent of the members of those societies." The "certain strategic respects" were enumerated as follows: (1) size of membership; (2) age composition and relationships of the membership through time; (3) composition by sex; (4) generational composition; (5) number of marital pairs; and (6) number of siblings. No matter what the variation of the ideal family and kinship structures, in practice the majority of the people in all societies have lived in families that have been virtually the same in these "strategic respects."

Levy noted three known ideal family types in terms of their vertical and horizontal proliferation. Vertical proliferation is the inclusion in the family unit of every living generation of a family either along male or females lines of descent. Horizontal proliferation is the inclusion in the family unit of all living offspring of one sex after marriage or adulthood plus living nonadult children. In the case of a married child, the spouse and any children are included in the family unit. The traditional Chinese family represents ideal proliferation, both vertical and horizontal, because it involves "representatives of as many generations as possible selected in terms of one sex line and as many siblings of one sex as possible plus their spouses and all their non-adult children" (p. 47). The intermediate form is represented by the stem family which involves maximum proliferation vertically, all living generations, but not horizontally. Under the stem family structure, all but one sibling leave the family of origin at marriage. The stem family then can be composed of as many generations as possible selected in terms of one sex line. It includes one sibling of the same sex in each generation, his spouse, and all his nonadult or unmarried children. The nuclear family is an example of a lack of both horizontal and vertical proliferation.

Levy agued that regardless of the ideal type of family in a society, the degree of proliferation, whether horizontal or vertical, is approximately the same. He applied his basic proposition to three different types of societies. His first type includes preindustrial societies which are "devoid of modern medical technology" and have extremely high mortality rates (p. 49). The high mortality rate in these societies means that the probabilities are low for either joint survival of several generations on a line of descent, or joint survival into adulthood of several siblings of the same sex. It restricts the proliferation of actual families regardless of the society's ideal type of family which is extended like that of the Chinese. Levy's second type includes societies which have "highly developed modern medical technologies as part of generally high levels of "modernization." " In these modern industrialized societies, minimal demographic limitations are operating upon family proliferation but little variation from the ideal family patterns occurs. The nuclear family has become universal both in ideal type and in actual practice. Since minimal demographic limitations are in operation, the limitations upon family proliferation are self-induced. It was Levy's contention (p. 57) that in the first type of society where the ideal and actual structures fail to coincide, certain levels of integration and stability exist. Levy further hypothesized that the "stability of the large scale ideal family structures inhered in the fact that those ideal conditions were not in fact approximated much more often than was compatible with special levels of kinship administrative virtuosity" (p. 58). As the products of modernization reduce the demographic limitations upon the family unit and it becomes larger with more children surviving and parents living longer, the state of integration and stability is disrupted. As a result of this disruption, pressures are created in the direction of a smaller family unit in order to regain integration and stability. The final result is found in the second type of society where the nuclear family becomes the ideal structure and the actual pattern in the majority of cases.

Levy's third type of society emcompasses the transitional period between the first and second type of societies. The societies are transitional in that they "have imported some modern medical technologies but have not yet achieved stable high levels of modernization in general respects" (Levy, 1965:45-49). In these transitional societies, recently achieved low levels of mortality created a greater range of variation in actual family structures. But Levy (p. 49) saw this occurring only in the short run because, in the long run, he pointed out that:

> Insofar as the ideal structures calling for extended proliferation vertically and horizontally in excess of the ideal structures of the nuclear family in fact are approximated by the actual structures, however, that approximation carries with it sources in the direction if the institutionalization of a family structure characterized by less vertical and horizontal proliferation.

In addition to the previously mentioned works which supported and, in some cases, helped suggest Levy's argument, a number of recent examinations have lent support to his proposals. Two works have tested his view utilizing a cross-cultural perspective. Using contemporary cross-national data, Burch (1967), in an initial examination, and Wozniak (1972), who updated Burch's study, observed that large residential families and extended families did not predominate in any of the societies studied (N = 27). They also argued that those nations which had the larger family size averages (4 to 6 persons) were examples of Levy's transitional societies; hence, these large averages did not contradict Levy's proposition. An earlier exploratory study conducted by the author (Seward, 1974) attempted to test Levy's argument historically. Family data were compared for the United States from two selected counties in 1850 to data reported by the census bureau in 1960. This study focused upon family size and found a difference between 1850 and 1960 of less than one individual per family, a mean difference of .72 persons and a median difference of .66 persons. Over 60 percent of the family units in the 1850 sample were composed of four members or less, making it impossible for the majority of family units to have formed the ideal extended type of family.

In this work examples of Levy's three types of societies will be observed as the American family is traced from the colonial period to the present. To this end Levy's first type of society will be considered equivalent to that period in the development of the United States that is determined to have been preindustrial. The transitional society he discussed will be identified as the period in the history of the United States in which the processes of industrialization and urbanization were developing. Finally, the third type of society discussed by Levy will be considered equivalent to the period after which maturity was reached, or the postindustrial period. The breakdown of the development of the United States into these three periods is dealt with as the data are presented.

The foregoing completes a survey of the studies which support the traditional perspective of the family going through numerous historical changes as a result of the process of industrialization and urbanization, and of the more recently developed perspective challenging this traditional contention. This work attempts to continue in the more critical orientation of the latter perspective in understanding family change and stability. Before continuing, a number of problems and limitations that are a part of the works reviewed should be discussed.

One problem is the lack of agreement about the meaning of the concepts that are a part of the generalization. The boundaries of the family unit and those variables that should be used to determine its boundaries often vary. Similar problems exist with regard to the concepts of industrialization and urbanization.

Another problem is the lack of quantitative data before the 1900s, and the important limitations of the available information. First, few complete records exist that deal with families before the turn of the century. Many of the intimacies and common behavior of family life were taken for granted and never recorded; this is also a contemporary problem. Certain events, behavior patterns, or incidents, because of their deviant or illicit nature, were left unrecorded. On the other hand some deviant or illicit acts which were more visible and especially those that came under the control of civil authorities were recorded. But

although these are available (e.g., court records), their representativeness is questionable. Usually only the phenomena that were
considered unusual, important, and at the same time acceptable
to the observer were recorded. Hence, the perspective of the
observer becomes an important variable. Some of the best
records of families have been preserved primarily because they
were part of a family business record, hence the economic
emphasis in family history (cf., Saveth, 1969:313-314). Also, most
available records are about families which were a part of the
upper social and economical segment of society.

Finally, a major problem of many works is the narrow focus
used in explaining family change. This is a result of the almost
universal acceptance of industrialization and urbanization as the
prime "cause" of social change over the last two centuries. Using
the components of the ecosystem as a guide, i.e., population,
organization, environment, and technology, this limited focus
can be observed. In the past, the concentration of arguments
stressed the effects of technology (industrialization) upon the
family and, to a lesser extent, the effect of urbanization. Recently,
the arguments have expanded to include other variables that
should be associated with family change. Many of these variables
are the result of work in the area of historical demography.
Additional variables of population have been noted and presented,
such as migration, sex ratio (cf., Moller, 1945:113-129), and the
mortality rate versus the birth rate (cf., Habakkuk, 1953:
117-133; Krause, 1958:164-188; P. Laslett, 1965a:582-594; Peterson, 1960:334-347; Potter, 1965:631-688). In the area of environment, such variables as the amount of natural resources, the fertility of the land (cf., Norton, 1971:433-452; Potter, 1965:631-688),
and the types of terrain have been presented. In the area of
organization, variables such as economic opportunities (cf.,
Habakkuk, 1953:117-133), inheritance systems (cf., Harris, 1969:
113-121), age at marriage (cf., Collver, 1963:86-96), ownership
of land and available land, residential propinquity (cf., Norton,
1972:433-452), birth control mechanisms, and occupational
systems have been presented. This is not meant to be an exhaus-
tive listing of variables, but merely a demonstration of the

variables that have been cited. This study utilizes some of these works and attempts to assess the relative importance and effect of some of these variables upon family change. This is a much broader approach than the sharp focus of many observers who have singled out one or two variables to account for most family change. The approach, however, is justified if it ascertains, at least to some degree, the effect or failure of these variables to explain change in a systematic analysis of the American family system.

This study has taken into account these problems and made an effort to deal with them. Several of them have been dealt with rather directly during the pursuit of the concerns listed at the beginning of this chapter.

Chapter 2

THE COLONIAL AMERICAN FAMILY

A Recent Documentation of Its Structure*

In attempts to describe and account for life (including family life) during the American colonial period, two elements have been emphasized. One is the importance of the European traditions that the colonists brought with them; the other is the distinctive environment they found in this new and undeveloped land. In most cases the emphasis has been upon the corrosive force of the latter element upon the imported European traditions. As Henretta (1971:379) stated: "A new type of society was created as the culture of the past was rendered irrelevant by the primitive logic of necessity, and as the contributing social and psychological bonds of the pre-modern world were dissolved by the corrosive forces of nature." Calhoun's (1919) work probably best presented this argument but the theme still is a popular one (cf., Adams, 1975:58-65; Martinson, 1970:13-38).

---

*Much of the work and data presented here were also used as the basis for a published paper entitled "The colonial family in America: toward a socio-historical restoration of its structure." *Journal of Marriage and the Family* 35 (February 1973): 58-70.

Developing along with this general view has been a stereotype portrayal of the family life that existed during the colonial period. In fact, this stereotypic image appears to be, in part, synonymous with what Goode (1963:6-7) termed "the classical family of Western nostalgia." The evidence for a majority of the aspects presented by this nostalgic traditional view is derived largely from "verbal data," such as diaries, sermons, novels, and other literary sources. In 1919 Arthur W. Calhoun published a social history of the American family which primarily used these literary sources, particularly those written by leading contemporaries for the colonial period. Calhoun's work presented the best summary of the family aspects that compose the traditional view. Potter (1965:647) even suggested that this stereotypic view was mainly derived from Calhoun. Although there were other earlier writers who presented a similar view (cf., Wertenbaker, 1929:182-187), Calhoun has been considered the primary progenitor of the traditional portrayal, and he has also been an antagonist in assaults upon the traditional portrayal of the colonial family. This role of Calhoun's was suggested by the dedication in a book by Gordon (1973): "To Arthur W. Calhoun, who started all of this."

Traditional View of the Colonial Family

The family during the colonial period was considered the most important social unit in society. Particularly in the New England area, which was under the influence of Puritanism, a strong emphasis was placed upon the family as the "corner-stone of society" (Potter, 1965:647). In fact, the attempt was made "to bring everyone under the authority of a family ruler," and the governmental system made every effort to aid the family rulers in the "proper exercise of their authority" (Martinson, 1970:17).

Most of the stereotypic portrayal of the colonial family related more appropriately to the New England colonies, but often very little distinction was made between the colonial regions. Although more recent attempts (Potter, 1965) have noted the differences between the New England, Mid-Atlantic, and Southern colonies, there has been general agreement that some of the basic family patterns were very similar. Thus much of what applies to New England family life also appears to apply to the middle colonies with only a slight modification (p. 652). The primary difference appears to have been that in the middle colonies there was less stress and more tolerance in regard to family life (Lantz and Snyder, 1969:36). Greater modifications of the traditional view seem appropriate for the Southern colonies, but even here the importance of the family's role in society was stressed (pp. 36-37). One problem that has plagued an analysis of the Southern colonies is the lack of statistical evidence. Even with recent developments it is still an important problem (Potter, 1965:662). Most of the data presented here are primarily limited to the New England area. But similarities between family life in all the colonies and that of other colonial regions mean that, to a limited extent, the results can be generalized. Attitudes toward marriage were associated with this general emphasis on the family's role in society. Marriage was the rule in New England and it was expected to occur at a young age. Unmarried women were looked upon with disapproval especially; single women beyond the age of twenty-five were referred to as a "thornbacks" (Martinson, 1970:30). Unmarried men were viewed with suspicion and, in some cases, almost categorized as suspected criminals. Since the wife-mother role was the major career opportunity open to women, and since women were in short supply, marriages were formed early and widows rapidly remarried. Two examples frequently cited in this regard are those of Cotton Mather, a famous Puritan preacher, and Judge S. Sewell. Mather "married a widow eight months after the death of his first wife" and Sewell "paid court, after the death of his first wife, to at least five widows, two of whom he married (the first of these dying within a year)" (Potter, 1965:647).

The fertility of married couples was extremely high and, in some cases, maternity was an annual event (p. 647). Of course these children grew up, married early, and were similarly productive. To support this view, claims of outstanding productivity are frequently cited. One example that Potter mentions (pp. 647

and 651) concerned a Maria Hagard, "who lived to be 100 years old in Rhode Island, [and] claimed 500 descendents; at her own death, 205 of these were still alive and a granddaughter of hers had herself been a grandmother for fifteen years." Death as a result of childbirth was cited as a frequent occurrence, and many young mothers were believed to have died as a result of child-bearing and/or overwork.

Mortality among infants was believed to be very high resulting in a small overall family size (children surviving). Again, Cotton Mather and Judge Sewell are frequently cited as examples. Out of Mather's fifteen children only two outlived him, and out of Sewell's fourteen children only three outlived him.

Until the past decade, this has been the stereotypic view of the colonial American family. Although the emphasis is upon the New England area (as well as the sources), the image has generally been applied to all of the colonies.

Since the 1960s, a number of scholars have been systematically challenging this stereotypic portrayal of the colonial American family. These recent works have particularly challenged five of the structural aspects of this earlier view. The characteristics which are the focus of this chapter include generational composition, number of children, family size, age at marriage, and infant mortality rate.

(1) The generational composition of the colonial family was viewed as being "extended" rather than "nuclear"—the implication being that a number of generations of kin, a number of siblings and their spouses were all a part of the family unit. This applied to both the residential pattern as well as the obligation pattern. Since the concern here is with the structural trends, the emphasis is upon the residential pattern.

(2) The number of children per family was expected to be quite large with childbirth often being an annual event. According to Calhoun (1919:87): "Large families were the rule. Families of ten to twelve children were common. Families of from twenty to twenty-five children were not rare enough to call forth expression of wonder."

(3) Total family size was quite large. The number of children per family was large. Combined with the "extended" nature of the family, this meant the total unit had a very large membership.

(4) Marriage occurred at a very early age in the colonial family. Although child marriages were not permitted, Calhoun (1919: 67) stated that women usually married at age sixteen or under and men at age twenty or under.

(5) The mortality rate for infants was particularly high (Calhoun, 1919:89). Calhoun noted that in the severe climate of New England, "the mortality rate of infants was frightful."

These points deal with some of the most important structural aspects of the colonial family, and recent data provide a new view in contrast to the view presented above. Although these aspects are the primary focus here, others will be mentioned.

New Research Approach for Old Data

Before preceding on to the "new" data, a review of the origins and techniques which have made possible a more accurate view is in order.

An important element in the recent developments in the study of the American colonial family has been the field of historical demography. As Greven (1967:438) observed, the "recent discovery of the family as an important subject of historical inquiry must lead, inevitably, to the discovery of the broader field of historical demography." Early American demographic history is just starting to be explored and the techniques of historical demography are proving, and should continue to prove, to be useful for early American socio-historical studies. A full account of historical demography's development is beyond the scope of this chapter, but may be obtained from Glass (1965), Wrigley (1966b), Henry (1968), and Hollingsworth (1969).

One of the most useful and popular techniques coming from the area of historical demography is family reconstitution. This technique was developed by Louis Henry (cf., Wrigley, 1966b: 153-154), a pioneer in French historical demography. Family reconstitution is the bringing together of scattered information about family members in a number of successive generations. It allows the demographic characteristics of the family to be described as fully as possible. These data are collected through a laborious procedure of compiling every available fragment of information about births, marriages, and deaths for all members of the family. A more detailed description of family reconstitution is presented by Wrigley (pp. 96-159). The results, when this technique is applied to a group of families in a community, are invaluable, as noted by works presented in this chapter that have used it (cf., Greven, 1966; Demos, 1968; Wells, 1971). The further use of this method in other communities and areas can help in providing "new" and hitherto inaccessible evidence from previously recorded but unused raw data. An excellent example of this is provided by Wrigley's (1966a:82-109) article on family limitation in preindustrial England.

Another useful technique for restoration is aggregative analysis. As Eversley (1966b:44-95) described it, aggregative analysis involves the accumulation, by months and years, of data from vital records—births, marriages, and deaths—for particular communities. On the basis of the data gathered, it is possible to restore evidence regarding the rates and variations of demographic characteristics over longer periods of time. Compared to family reconstitution, aggregative analysis is a less time consuming procedure but, at the same time, it lacks the completeness of the former technique. The application and usefulness of aggregative analysis in the colonial family's restoration can be seen in Lockridge's (1966) work on Dedham, Massachusetts. Using both techniques on the same population can also be advantageous (Norton, 1971:433). It must be mentioned, however, that there are important limitations inherent in these procedures, especially that of family reconstitution, that cannot be ignored when using data resulting from their application (Norton, 1971:439; Vinovskis, 1971:570-590).

These techniques have played an important role in a number of studies which have presented data that challenge the traditional view of the American colonial family. As a result, there is a great deal of support for a new image of the colonial American family.

Data for a New View

GENERATIONAL COMPOSITION

There has been a growing amount of material challenging the traditional view of the generational composition of the colonial family. In fact, the assumption that the colonial family was "extended" has come under much attack despite its widespread support. In addition to the views of Calhoun and Wertenbaker, Greenfield (1967:312) observed that it is "generally viewed in sociological theory" that the "small nuclear family found in Western Europe and the United States" is the "consequence of the urban-industrial revolution." Furthermore, the "extended" family was the expected form that preceded the urban-industrial revolution. Greenfield (1967), through an excellent use of comparative and historical techniques, challenges this assumed relationship between the family and the urban-industrial revolution and even suggests that the small nuclear family might possibly have helped produce industrialization.

Greenfield advances the important thought (1967:322) that the "small nuclear family was brought to the United States from Great Britain by its earliest settlers." He bases this on Arensberg's contention (1955:1149) that the "'nuclear' or 'democratic' family . . . came with [the] Yankees from England." But there is also additional support for this view. In his study of the aristocracy between 1558 and 1641, Stone (1967:269) noted there is a lack of evidence that the "sixteenth century household had taken the form of an extended family." There appeared, in fact, to be little "encouragement for younger sons to remain home, and daughters were almost invariably married off at an early age" (Stone, 1967:269). Laslett and Harrison (1963:167), in their study of seventeenth century Clayworth and Cogenhoe, found that the family was not extended, because in most cases the "household did not ordinarily contain more generations than two, [and] . . . living with in-laws or relatives was on the whole not to be expected. . . . Most important is the rule that it was unusual, very unusual, to find two married couples within the same family group." P. Laslett (1969) expanded the geographical coverage of these conclusions in a later work. He supported the contention that the family form brought to the new world by the English settlers was "nuclear" in nature rather than "extended." Thus, if the extended family was typical in the colonies it must have been because of indigenous elements in the new world.

But based upon recently completed work, the "nuclear" family was also typical in the American colonies in contrast to the stereotype. A number of studies completed since 1965 of the colonial family conclude that the extended structure was the exception rather than the rule. Demos (1965:279) noted that in the Plymouth colony "there were not extended families at all, in the sense of 'under the same roof.' " Using family wills as a source, he observed "that married brothers and sisters never lived together in the same house," and that "as soon as a young man becomes bethrothed, plans were made for the building, or purchase, of his own house." In his study of Dedham, Massachusetts, between 1636 and 1736, Lockridge (1966:343) observed that "80 percent of adult, married men had their own house. . . . [hence there was] not extensive doubling-up of two families in one house . . . [and] it was most unusual for married fathers with married sons to live together in an extended family group."

In his study of the seventeenth century family structure in Andover, Massachusetts, Greven (1966:254-255) described what he termed a *"modified extended family*—defined as a kinship group of two or more generations living within a single community in which the dependence of the children upon their parents continues after the children have married and are living under a separate roof." Greven's findings are not, however, at odds with the previous findings. What he termed the *modified extended family* refers to the family of interaction or obligation and, to be consistant with the other works, we must use the family of residence as a basis for the family unit. Hence to distinguish between an "extended" and a "nuclear" family unit, the generational composition is considered for those persons who are related by blood, marriage, or adoption and who share the same dwelling unit. The importance of the interpersonal relationships between all kin, whether residing in the same dwelling unit or not—the family of interaction—cannot yet be dealt with in quantitative terms. Thus if the definition of family of residence is applied to Greven's families, the difference in structure disappears. This distinction made, the family structure as described by Greven is, in fact, nuclear, as are the families in the works previously cited.

In a later study by Demos (1968:44) of colonial Bristol, Rhode Island, he supported the predominance of the "nuclear" family by observing that "married adults normally lived with their own children and *apart* from all other relatives." Together, these works provide evidence based upon quantitative data to challenge the contention of the predominance of the "extended" family in the colonial period.

NUMBER OF CHILDREN PER FAMILY

Another view under close scrutiny is that the number of children per family was quite large. It is true that colonial families, on the average, had more children than families of the present day. However, the difference between these two periods has been much exaggerated, and certainly the difference is much less than indicated by Calhoun. Indeed, if we look at Demos' statistics (1968), there appears to be little variance in the average number of children from the present figure. Demos (1968:45) reported the mean number of children per family in colonial Bristol for 1689 as 3.27 and the median as 3.04. Only two families of those surveyed by Demos had more than seven children. If the mean reported by Demos (3.27) is compared to means reported by the United States Census Bureau (1963b:21; 1973a:23) for 1960 and 1970 (1.54 for both), the difference (1.73) is much less than might be presumed. Regardless of whether this figure is considered to be a significant difference, the figures presented by Demos (1968) certainly challenge the image of the typical colonial family as one having a large number of children.

However, in various works there are large discrepancies which should be noted in the figures reported for the number of children per colonial family. In an earlier work Demos (1965:270) reported that in the Plymouth colony there was "an average of seven to eight children per family who actually grew to adulthood." If the children who died before the age of twenty-one are included in Demos' sample, the average is raised to eight and nine children. In a recent work dealing only with eighteenth century Quakers, Wells (1971:74-75) reported the average number of children per family as 5.69. Other figures include the following: Greven (1966:238) for Andover, Massachusetts—an average of 8.5 children per family, with 7.2 children in these families reaching the age of twenty-one; Lockridge (1966:330) for Dedham, Massachusetts—an average of 4.64 children for each family; Higgs and Stettler (1970:286-287) for ten different New England towns—an average of seven children per family; Norton (1971:444) for Ipswich, Massachusetts—a mean number of 4.3 children per family, where "the date of the end of union is known" and a mean of 6.4 children for those families that were "technically complete," that is, where the wife remained married at least up to the age of 45, or where the union lasted at least 27 years; Smith (1972:177) for Hingham, Massachusetts presented a mean number of 6.53 children per family, which is the overall mean for six marriage cohorts that cover a period from 1641 to 1800, but there are significant variations from this average, especially the 1691-1715 cohort, which had the lowest mean with 4.61 children per family. Hence, even if we accept the highest reported averages, the stereotype is challenged. Still a wide discrepancy exists between the various figures that must be explored.

One explanation might be that the various figures are unique for the particular town or area studied. Thus, just as it is impossible to describe accurately colonial life based only upon observations by Benjamin Franklin and a few others, it is also impossible to generalize and relate from the findings of one town in colonial America to an entire area or era. In an attempt to overcome this problem, Higgs and Stettler (1970) collected data

from a number of different towns. They observed that differences
between towns existed and must be realized and expected. They
noted (1970:289), for example, that the average number of
children per family varied from "a low of 5.19 in Malden to a high
of 7.76 in Brookfield." The difference (2.57) in the average number of children is still much smaller than the difference (5.23)
between figures reported by Greven (1966) and Demos (1968).
Geographical differences in sampling, then, may be a partial
explanation for this discrepancy but do not suffice as a complete
explanation.

Another factor that accounts for part of the discrepancy is a
decline during the colonial period in completed fertility. Smith
(1972:177-179) noted a decline in completed fertility in the
eighteenth century as compared to the seventeenth century with
the lowest rate recorded by those women marrying at the beginning of the eighteenth century (1691-1715). As Smith suggests,
this is a pattern not unique to Hingham and it is, to some degree,
supported by the rates presented by the other studies. The higher
means, in most cases, come from studies of seventeenth century
populations, and the lower means usually come from studies of
eighteenth century populations. This decline in completed
fertility is a factor in the discrepancy and must be explored
further. But there is a simpler explanation for the wide differences.

The main reason for the widespread range of figures presented
above is the use of varying operational definitions determining
the number of children per family. The biggest difference results
from the use by observers of the colonial family unit of dissimilar
time perspectives. Currently the United States Census Bureau
(1963b:xxiv; 1973a:ix) reports the number of children per family
as only those children residing in a household—family of residence—at the time of enumeration. Thus children who have left
home, died, or are yet to be born are not counted. Included in
the calculation of the average number of children per family are
childless couples, who were usually not a part of colonial studies'
figures. This represents a crosssectional view of the family and
its characteristics. With only one exception—Demos (1968)—all

of the studies mentioned above take a longitudinal perspective
with regard to number of children per family.

Utilization of the longitudinal perspective means observing
the completed family while noting the number of children in each
family. The completed family includes a husband, his wife, and
any children born into their union. Although this has been the
most common operational definition of the family used to determine the number of children and family size, there are some
unique qualifications employed by some researchers that should
be noted. In his earlier study, for example, Demos (1965:270)
used only "families in which both parents lived at least to age
50, or else if one parent died, the other quickly remarried."
Higgs and Stettler (1970:284) included only families for which
continuous residence in the same town was recorded throughout
the entire childbearing period. Also note the difference (2.1)
between families that were "technically complete" and those
families where the date a union ended was known, as reported
by Norton (1971:444). But even the lower mean (4.1) is overstated
as compared to contemporary figures because it is still based
upon a longitudinal perspective, and because of restrictions on
the sample (Norton, 1971:443).

It becomes obvious that the number of children per family
derived from an operational definition based upon the completed
family gives us a much larger number than the cross-sectional
perspective. This is not only the case for the colonial era but
also for the United States today. With the use of additional
limitations, like those used by Demos (1965), Higgs and Stettler
(1970), and Norton (1971), a representative sample cannot be
obtained from the areas studied. Higgs and Stettler (1970:284,
288) admit that their estimates of the number of children and
family size are overstated. Certainly overstatement must occur in
all those works using a similar type of operational definition.
Yet, because of the uneven recording of the data, a qualification
stipulating the use of only those families for which complete
data exist seems to be necessary. In addition to overstatement
resulting from sample qualifications, smaller, mobile families
were less likely to generate the necessary successive birth, death,
and marriage registrations which would assure inclusion in the

sample. The fact that those small, mobile families had a lower probability of being included in a sample supports the contention that samples dealing only with completed families—using the longitudinal perspective—are unrepresentative and have overstated figures.

Another related factor can partially account for the higher averages when dealing with completed families. Most studies that deal with the completed family include in the sample only parents or couples with children. Only these parents were used in the calculation of the average number of children per family. Thus, families (couples) without children were not included in this computation and, as a result, the average reported was additionally overstated. Wells (1971:74-75) provided a partial exception in his calculation of figures on the number of children per family. He did include couples without any children but eliminated couples when the bride's age did not fall "within the normal limits of the childbearing stage of life." Thus Wells' figures are still overstated but not as badly as those who excluded all childless couples. It should be noted that the figures reported by Wells are modest in comparison to those reported by others. Also his figures are more comparable to current census data that include parents with children, childless couples, and married couples before, during, and after childbearing age in the calculation of averages.

The only colonial data comparable to contemporary census data are provided by Demos' (1968) figures based upon a census taken of colonial Bristol in 1689. These data indicate the least variance between the contemporary and colonial figures (for figures see above). Although differences would still be expected if we could derive comparable, cross-sectional data from the other colonial studies, the average number of children per family would be reduced significantly. The conclusion must be that the number of children per family has been much exaggerated and that the actual number of children per family is not too different from the present figures.

FAMILY SIZE

The assumption of a large number of children, together with the presumption of the "extended" nature of the colonial family, accounts for the widespread image of large colonial family units. But in regard to overall family size it seems reasonably clear that the size of the colonial American family was much smaller than presumed. First, we noted the restricted nature—only two generations—of the family of residence in regard to generational composition. Second, the actual number of children in the colonial family unit at any given time appears to have been smaller than previously presumed. The exaggerated figures presented for family size, when applying the U.S. Census' present definition, appear to be the result of most authors using a limited number of completed families to determine overall family size.

An additional element which produced an exaggerated family size was the presence of nonrelatives in the family's household. These were often counted as family members. An extreme example was presented by Demos (1965:285) using the household of Samuel Fuller. At Fuller's death in 1633, there were nine people in his household; five of these were not family members. In addition to his wife, son, and nephew, there were two servants, a ward, and two "additional children." The "additional children" had been sent from other families to the Fuller household for education. The inclusion of wards, servants, borders, resident employees, and others as part of overall family size existed in preindustrial England as well, as noted by Laslett and Harrison (1963:167-169) and P. Laslett (1965a:589). It is noteworthy that the practice of counting all households members as members of the same family of residence, regardless of their relationship to one another, was continued by the United States Census Bureau (1949:18) until 1930.

Considering only those studies of colonial families where the exaggeration factors are controlled or eliminated, family size appears to have been relatively small. Lockridge (1966:343) taking into account only parents and children, derived from lists of houses an average family size of six for Dedham, a little under six for Medfield, and less than five for Salem. In colonial

Bristol, where Demos (1968:45) also eliminated all servants and counted only parents and children, the average family size was 5.32. Demos' figures from Bristol resulted from a fairly complete (and apparently unique) census taken in 1689.

During the colonial period the compiling of lists for military and tax purposes (usually including only adult males) was quite common, but the 1689 census contained a constituency of all household members and categorized them according to family and nonfamily positions (p. 43). Only one copy of the census still survives and, unfortunately, no clue exists as to the reason it was taken in the first place. Nevertheless, it does provide cross-sectional data on family membership in a colonial community. Because of this, the data are comparable to those presented in the following chapters. The document included the following four columns: head of household, under which the name was listed; wife, children, and servants. Under the last three headings the appropriate figure was listed. Using the data provided, the distribution and average size of the colonial Bristol families in 1689 are presented in Table 2.1.

Demos (1968:50-51) presented similar data for Bristol from an official census taken in 1774 for the whole colony of Rhode Island. Unfortunately, the distinction between family and non-family positions was not made in this census. The only helpful discrimination made was between white inhabitants and Black and Indian inhabitants of the households. The latter were presumably servants or slaves. The data derived from this later census are presented in Table 2.1. The "families" included the white inhabitants of 193 households plus one "independent family of 3 Negroes." The fact that there were still some white servants in 1774 means that the later figures are exaggerated. Demos (pp. 54-55) estimated that probably 30 percent or more of the "families" included white servants.

The data in Table 2.1 certainly do not support the existence of large families during the colonial era. At the same time it is ridiculous to assume that statistics from this one community represent all of the colonies in North America. However, the data for North America presented by Greven (1972) in Laslett

Table 2.1: Number of Families, and Percentage Distribution
by Size for Colonial Bristol, 1689 and 1774

Size of Family	1689	1774*
All units	68	194
Percentage	100.0	100.0
2 persons	8.8	12.9
3 persons	14.7	15.0
4 persons	16.2	14.4
5 persons	17.7	9.8
6 persons	13.2	11.9
7 persons	11.8	11.3
8 persons	8.8	8.3
9 persons	5.9	5.7
10 persons	1.5	6.7
11 persons or more	1.5	3.1
Modal size	5.00	3.00
Median size	5.08	5.29
Mean size	5.32	5.61

*White servants are included as family members.
Source: Demos (1968: 41-54).

and Wall's cross-cultural comparison of household and family
composition over the last 500 years seems to preclude the likelihood that family size was much larger during the colonial period
than Demos' data stipulated. Greven presented data from the
only known censuses for the colonial era in addition to the 1774
Rhode Island census used by Demos that makes a houshold
family distinction—Massachusetts in 1764 and eleven of the
United States in 1790. The family size figures he presented (pp.
550-552) are larger than Demos' but the differences are not very
great. For example, the largest figure reported by Greven (6.04
for Maryland in 1790) is only 0.7 more than Demos' lowest figure
reported in Table 2.1. A thorough examination of his data
sources suggests several elements which result in inflated figures
in all cases (cf., Seward, 1977:7-12). For example, unrelated
individuals who shared the same dwelling (including slaves,
servants, lodgers, or boarders) were all counted as one "family"
unit. Eliminating this as well as other exaggeration factors would
reduce Greven's family size figures to a level that in several cases
would be lower than those reported by Demos.

Demos (1968) argued that his figures were inflated as well because they were biased toward larger families in both cases. Even though the 1689 census included only family members, the figures were prejudiced in that a substantial proportion of the couples (parents) in Bristol were at or near middle age and, therefore, more likely to exhibit large families (p. 49). Although a considerable number of young couples were present, there was almost a complete absence of elderly couples. For the 1774 data an age group bias apparently does not exist, but the inclusion of white servants disposes the figures toward a larger average size. Out of a population of 1088 residing in households, 224 people were single and over 16 years of age. Demos considered a certain proportion of these individuals to be potential white servants. By eliminating them from the total number of individuals in family units, Demos (pp. 54-55) reduced the family mean from 5.61 to 5.03. This lower figure is probably more accurate than the mean presented in Table 2.1. Some support for the lower figure was also presented earlier when an overall decline in fertility during the eighteenth century was noted.

Keeping in mind these biases and the limited representativeness of the data, the measures of central tendency still indicate much smaller families than previously expected for the majority of the population. In both the 1689 and 1774 censuses, most family units were composed of five members or less. The distributions for the two periods were similar with most change occurring at the opposite ends of the distribution. The increase in two person families in 1774 may be due to a larger population of elderly couples, and the increase in families with 7 or more persons may be the result of the presence of white servants.

Finally, in comparing Lockridge's and Demos' figures with the average family size in the United States in 1960 (3.65) and 1970 (3.57) [Bureau of Census, 1963b:465; 1973a:55], we find a difference from 2.4+ to less than 1.7+ persons per family. Hence, there is little support for the belief that large families dominated in the colonial period since the average family at that time did not appear to be much larger than that of the contemporary family. More detailed comparisons for family size throughout American history will be provided in later chapters.

AGE OF MARRIAGE

The age estimates suggested by Calhoun appear to be completely erroneous when compared to a consensus of recent works.
Not only is the colonial marriage age much higher than that stated
by Calhoun, but most of the ages reported for both men and
women are higher than those of the present day. Demos (1965:
275) reported that in the Plymouth colony the average age at
first marriage for men dropped from 27.0 to 24.6 years; for
women it increased from 20.6 to 22.3 years. His study included
people born before 1600 and those born by 1700, and the resul-
tant statistics were divided into twenty-five year groups based
upon date of birth. Norton (1971:445) found a similar pattern in
Ipswich in regard to age at first marriage but the age levels
occurred approximately half a century later than in the Plymouth
colony. Lockridge (1966:331) reported that from 1640 to 1690
the average age at first marriage in Dedham was 25.5 years for
men and 22.5 years for women. Greven (1966:240) observed
nearly identical results in Andover. In Hingham, although the
overall trend was the same, the highest ages at first marriage for
both sexes increased initially and reached their highest level
from 1691 to 1715 (Smith, 1972:177). For colonial Bristol,
Demos (1968:55) reported the lowest ages at first marriage of all
the colonial studies yet cited. For those couples in colonial
Bristol who married before 1750, the men had an average age
of 23.9 and the women had an average age of 20.5. For those
couples who married after 1750, the men had an average age of
24.3 and the women an average age of 21.1. Higgs and Stettler
(1970:285) report ages remarkably similar to those reported by
Demos for Bristol.

A comparison of the above figures to current data is problematical because age at marriage is reported by the United States
Census Bureau in medians, not means or averages. Demos'
(1968) study of colonial Bristol is the exception since he reported
both the mean and the median age. His data are presented in
Table 2.2 along with other colonial and more current data. The
table shows that figures presented by Demos in his 1968 study
are markedly similar to those of the contemporary period.

Table 2.2: Age at First Marriage: Figures from Colonial Studies
and the U.S. Census Bureau[a]

Time of Marriage	Age of Men		Age of Women	
1600s	Mean	Median	Mean	Median
Before 1624[b] (Plymouth)	27.0		20.6	
1640-1690[c] (Dedham)	25.5		22.5	
Before 1691[d] (Hingham)	27.4		22.0	
1700s				
1691-1715[d] (Hingham)	28.4		24.7	
Before 1750[e] (Bristol)	23.9	22.4	20.5	20.3
After 1750[e] (Bristol)	24.3	23.8	21.1	20.8
1800s				
1890[f] (U.S.)		26.1		22.0
1900s				
1900[f] (U.S.)		25.9		21.9
1920[f] (U.S.)		24.6		21.2
1940[f] (U.S.)		24.3		21.5
1950[f] (U.S.)		22.8		20.3
1960[g] (U.S.)		22.8		20.3
1970[h] (U.S.)		23.4		20.7

a. Data for the 1600s and 1700s have been selected from a number of studies dealing with families residing in colonial communities.
b. Source: Demos (1965:275).
c. Source: Lockridge (1966:333).
d. Source: Smith (1972:177).
e. Source: Demos (1968:55).
f. Source: United States: Bureau of Census (1960a:15).
g. Source: United States: Bureau of Census (1965:3).
h. Source: United States: Bureau of Census (1973b:1).

Considering the discrepancy between the ages reported by
the various colonial family studies, we should first note that the
lower ages presented by Demos (1968) and Higgs and Stettler
(1970:285) contrast with the higher ages reported by Lockridge
(1966), Greven (1966), and Demos (1965). The difference is
related to the century in which the births of the individuals in
the sample occurred. The group with the higher marriage ages
for men and women used samples of individuals born in the
seventeenth century, while the group with lower marriage ages

used individuals born in the eighteenth century. Norton (1971: 445) and Smith (1972:177), whose data present figures for both centuries, support these trends. For men, the average age at first marriage was higher in the seventeenth century and lower in the eighteenth century; for women, the average age fluctuated from lower in the seventeenth century, higher around the end of the seventeenth century and the beginning of the eighteenth century, somewhat lower during the middle of the eighteenth century, to slightly higher toward the end of the eighteenth century. Smith (1972:176-177) cited a number of additional sources which confirm this trend.

There appears to be a return to a higher age for both sexes in the nineteenth century, as represented by the 1890 data in Table 2.2. These figures show a noticeable similarity to the higher ages for those individuals born in the seventeenth century. Although the former presents a median age and the latter a mean age, at this point there is little basis to suppose that a much greater difference would result if the statistics were the same. From the Demos (1968) figures, it can be observed that when both the mean and the median are reported, the difference seems to be rather small. The mean age will usually be a higher figure than the median because the mean will be affected by those individuals who marry comparatively late while the median will not be affected as long as these individuals lie above the median (cf., Boalt, 1965:66-67).

A tentative fluctuation pattern for age at marriage emerges. Age at first marriage was quite high in the seventeenth century colonies with the period toward the end of the seventeenth and beginning of the eighteenth having the highest reported ages. The age at marriage for females varies a bit from this pattern in that a very low age is reported for the early 1600s. This also results in females having a larger range of ages for the 1600s than males. The trend for the eighteenth century for both sexes is toward a lower level for age at marriage. Of interest is that these lower age levels are remarkably similar to the levels obtained during the present century, i.e., for 1950, 1960, and 1970. During the nineteenth century there occurred a marriage age akin to the high age levels reported for the colonial seventeenth century. Since 1890 there has been an overall pattern of decline in the ages of first marriage for both sexes. Age of females increased slightly in 1940 but the 1950s produced a fairly drastic drop in the age levels for females as well as males, possibly as a result of World War II. The age levels for 1970 may indicate a reversal of this declining trend.

A number of factors have been cited as determining age levels at marriage in the colonial period. The high ages for men and low ages for women at first marriage during the first decades of settlement in the seventeenth century have been attributed to a severely imbalanced sex ratio (Henretta, 1971:387; Smith, 1972: 176). Moller's (1945:113-153) study of passengers on ships coming to New England further supported this view. But as Norton (1971:445-446) noted, the Puritans emphasized that Massachusetts—where the majority of the communities studied and cited here are located—must be colonized by family units rather than by single men. For Ipswich an excess of males occurred for only a brief period after it was founded. Thus the importance of an imbalanced sex ratio for age at marriage was limited to the early decades of the 1600s. Norton suggests that economic considerations, particularly the demand for male labor, were important in determining age levels at marriage. In the eighteenth century the role of certain "external Pressures"— limited geographical expansion, military threat from the Indians and French, inheritance systems, migration, and overcrowded towns—upon marital age patterns have been emphasized (cf., Henretta, 1971:389-391; Smith, 1972:176-180).

The higher age levels for the seventeenth century could also be the result of stronger parental control over marriage. Hence the decline during the following century could indicate the decline of parental control over marriage. Support for this comes from the work of Smith (1973a; 1973b) in his study of Hingham, Massachusetts from the midseventeenth century to the mid-nineteenth century. Smith uses several demographic indices, one of which is age at marriage, to support his contention of declining parental power and/or the declining importance of the family of orientation. Smith uses age at marriage as an independent variable, rather than as a dependent variable, but the evidence he provides suggests the utility of reversing the causal direction of the relationship in this discussion.

As Smith (1973a:421) notes, age at marriage data are very important because marriage is an important transition point for an individual when he leaves the family of orientation to begin a family of procreation. The more control the family of orientation has, the more it will influence the timing of this transitional point.

Since sons did not usually share the parental dwelling unit or remain a part of the parental economic unit after marriage, parents, usually fathers, "had something to lose—either economic resources or unpaid labor services—by the early marriage of their sons" (p. 423). Marriage meant a release from a dependent status and its implied obligation for unmarried sons. In cases where sons remained part of the parental economic unit after marriage, they could be kept in a fairly dependent state for a long period of time after their marriage. Greven (1966: 244-245) noted this pattern, particularly for the eldest or oldest sons, in his study of Andover. During the colonial period farming communities like Andover required all the labor they could get. Sons were expected to provide labor services for as long as a father deemed necessary. Of course, in exchange for this prolonged contribution by sons, the sons were probably promised land in return. If sons followed this pattern they became dependent upon paternal assistance in order to marry. As a result, the age at marriage for sons was delayed. In the case of Andover (p. 243), the ages are similar to (and in some cases even higher than) the levels reported for the 1600s in Table 2.2.

In Andover the dependence of sons upon parental assistance was even extended after marriage. After marriage sons were frequently allowed to build homes upon their father's land but the father usually kept legal control of the land until his death.

When there was little land or too many sons, the better (or most of the) land was usually promised to the eldest sons (Smith, 1973a:423). The eldest sons (first and second born) were, on the average, married at a younger age than younger sons. A contributing factor must have been the father's ability to keep his older sons in a dependent position even after marriage by withholding legal control of their promised land. For the younger sons the promise of land was less frequent and important, but they were still dependent upon parental assistance to marry. Because the relationship between a father and his younger sons was less binding, the best way to assure continued services was to postpone marriage as long as possible. In Andover, when younger sons got married, they were usually over two years older than first born sons (Greven, 1966:243).

Smith (1973a:423) tested the control of parents over marriage by comparing the age at marriage for sons of men who died early to the sons of men who lived to an old age. If parental (more specifically, paternal) control was strong, the former group should marry at a younger age; as parental control diminished, these differences should disappear. For those sons born during the seventeenth century and most of the eighteenth century, the expected difference was found. Sons whose fathers died early married younger (1.16 years) than sons whose fathers lived longer. This difference might seem small, but, as Smith noted, it is bigger than the differences found between the marriage ages for first born sons versus younger sons, or for the sons of wealthy parents versus less wealthy parents.

At the end of the eighteenth century and continuing into the nineteenth century this age difference between sons whose fathers either died early or lived longer diminished. In fact, for certain segments of this period the difference was in an opposite direction. The implication is the diminishing importance of parental control over age at marriage for sons.

Smith (pp. 424-425) also observed the age at marriage for daughters to support his contention. Traditionally, daughters have been considered more subject to parental control in regard to marriage than sons. The evidence for the colonial period suggests the existence of an intermediate pattern "between total control of young women by their parents and substantive premarital autonomy for women" (p. 424). Smith argued that the more parental control held over daughters, the stronger the tendency to marry them off in their order of birth, starting with the eldest. The less control exhibited by parents, the more irregular the sequence of the sisters' marriages should become. Using age at marriage to establish the sequence of marriage, Smith found "a marked increase in the proportions of daughters who fail to marry in order of sibling position after the middle of the eighteenth century" (p. 425). This trend continued indicating that fewer and fewer daughters were not being "married off."

Another use made by Smith of data concerning the age of daughters at marriage (pp. 425-426) was to compare the relationship between wealth of parents and marriage age. If the transmission of wealth was important in society, daughters from wealthier families should marry earlier than daughters of less wealthy parents. When women were no longer expected to provide economic resources for their future husbands, this expected pattern should disappear. This is supported by the existence of an inverse relationship between wealth and marriage age for those daughters born to marriages between 1721 and 1780. However, for daughters born to marriages between 1781 and 1840 the reverse of this pattern is found, indicating the lack of importance given economic considerations and suggesting a decline in parental control. Through the use of age at marriage statistics, Smith suggested the reduction of parental control over the marriages of both daughters and sons. Thus the reduction of parental control was an important influence in the decline of the marriage age levels during the eighteenth century.

As with the tentative fluctuation pattern in marriage age levels suggested by Table 2.2, data on the marriage age patterns for the colonial period and, in particular, an understanding of the factors determining these patterns are fragmentary, although they do provide researchers with a basis for further investigation.

In addition, higher age at marriage for colonial women, as these studies appear to indicate, has implications for the birth rate and family size. A higher age at marriage for women is a form of family limitation (cf., Wrigley, 1966a:82-109) which reduces the birth rate because the number of birth potential years is shortened. As Smith (1972:178) noted, 43.3 percent of the decline in completed marital fertility for his 1691-1715 marriage cohort can be accounted for by an increase in female age at marriage.

INFANT MORTALITY RATE

Calhoun and others assumed that the infant mortality rate was quite high during the colonial period. However, several other works challenge this stereotypic view of the colonial family, even without data. If the number of children per family—completed families—is much less than expected, the majority of children born must survive to maintain a family unit that will continue from generation to generation. Furthermore, the fact that marriage was occurring at a much later age than assumed reduces the number of children that can be born. These two factors would seem to suggest the probability of a lower infant mortality rate than previously assumed.

The infant mortality rates reported by the various recent works are quite low, but each author notes the tentative nature of these findings. Demos (1965:271) observed that the rate of infant mortality for Plymouth was "relatively low" with only one child in five dying before the age of twenty-one. Because the exact date of death frequently cannot be established, Demos suggested that it is more accurate to speak of infant and child mortality together. This would apply to the other works as well. Potter (1965:656, 658-660), in a recalculation of data from New Jersey for the latter part of the eighteenth century, found "an astonishingly low infant mortality rate." Greven (1966:237) found in Andover that only 15.7 percent of the children whose births were ascertained died before the age of twenty-one. Norton (1971:442) found in Ipswich "strikingly low" infant and child mortality rates even after correcting for underrecording.

One major problem that particularly complicates infant mortality data for the colonial period is underrecording. As Lockridge (1966:329) observed, it is "known that still-born infants and infants who died within two or three days of birth were not recorded." Norton (1971:439-443) estimated that 33 percent of all infant deaths were not registered. Yet even after correcting for underrecording, applying estimates and techniques proscribed by Henry et al., and using family reconstitution to check upon the overall level of mortality derived from aggregative analysis, Norton found the mortality rates for Ipswich to be quite low. When family reconstruction is used to calculate mortality rates, only the mortality of married adults and, usually, only those children that remain in the family of residence can be studied. Although most recent works note a lower infant mortality rate than previously presumed, the data are limited to approximate levels of infant mortality.

One explanation that has received some support argues that elements in the colonial environment reduced the probability of a high infant mortality rate. Potter (1965:663) and Klingaman (1971:555) described the food supply for the colonies as generally adequate and increasingly abundant. In his review of mortality rates for Dedham and Watertown, Lockridge (1966:336) noted that these towns went through a century of life "substantially" free of disasters which could have cut deeply into the ranks of the population. This is in sharp contrast to the demographic crises experienced in similar European villages for the same period. Noting the lack of disease and hunger in these towns, Lockridge (1966:337) believed that it was "quite possible that the new land had substantial gifts to offer and freedom to bestow other than the freedom from Anglican persecutions." Norton (1971) suggested that the population growth and family size for Ipswich was not a result of high levels of fertility, but a consequence of low levels of mortality. Two factors that Norton (p. 448) cited for these low levels of mortality are the generally higher level of nutrition and a decrease in deaths resulting from infectious diseases, particularly epidemic diseases.

In Ipswich evidence of deaths due to famine was strikingly absent. Out of all of the deaths (237) for which a cause was given only one was attributed to starvation, and the same pattern is supported by the evidence from other towns. Famine was apparently only regarded as a serious threat during the very early years of settlement. Some occasional reports of scurvy and rickets, both of which are nutritional deficiency diseases, were found in the New England colonies but they were not considered to be major causes of death (p. 449).

A more important cause in reduced mortality than good nutrition was the apparent "marked decrease" in deaths resulting from infectious diseases. The primary role of infectious diseases in the high death rates of the past has been noted by McKeown and Brown (1955) and McKeown and Record (1962). The incidence of infection is essentially determined by environmental conditions (pp. 119-129). Hence, high mortality rates are "very sensitive" to improvements in the environment. Even slight improvements in environmental conditions can provide substantial improvement in the mortality rate. As Norton (1971: 449) stated, the colonization of America represented a dramatic improvement of the environmental conditions for the colonists. Their new environment was much less conducive to infectious disease than the environment from which they came. McKeown and Brown (1955:136), in fact, contended that the rapid population growth in the American colonies resulted from a "relatively low incidence of infectious disease in a thinly populated country." They also suggested that "the much publicized risk of death from violence was almost certainly less serious than the risk of death from infection in the old [country]."

The risk of contracting an infectious disease for an individual was much lower in the colonies than in most areas of Europe (Norton, 1971:449-450). First, there were fewer sources of infection and, second, once an infection was introduced, the rate of its spread was hampered. No evidence exists of infections being contracted from the indigenous population by the colonists. This means that all infections had to be imported. During the early colonial period, contact with England was sporadic and infrequent. The length of sailing time necessary for the trip probably allowed most shipboard epidemics to exhaust themselves before the colonies were reached. In the eighteenth century when trips were more frequent, the number of ships and passengers increased, and the sailing time was reduced. The intervals between epidemics were "decreased regularly and markedly."

Even when infections were introduced into the colonies, the environmental conditions were against the propagation of disease. Norton (p. 450) described these conditions for colonial Massachusetts: Its sparsely populated country with no substantial transportation network was simply incapable of "supporting many epidemic diseases or of allowing the inevitable, rapid or wide spread of an epidemic." Again this pattern changed during the eighteenth century for older coastal communities as the size of land holdings decreased. Other indications pointed to the "overcrowded" nature, by American standards, of these towns. An increase in population density usually increases the number of infecting sources as well as the number of persons in risk of infection. This increase in population density was probably also related to the rise of mortality in the eighteenth century.

Another factor in favor of the colonists was that once the infection had been contracted, the chances for survival were much better than in Europe. Chances for survival are dependent upon general standards of health for which the level of nutrition is an important part (McKeown and Brown, 1955). Nutrition is more important to mortality from infectious disease than the incidence of the disease, and the apparent better nutritional level of the colonists helped reduce mortality.

In summary, a number of conditions provided an improved environment in regard to mortality for the colonists—there were fewer sources of infection (all had to be imported), a decreased rate of the spread of infection (sparse population), and greater survival chances once the infection was contracted. Furthermore, as these conditions changed, the mortality rates increased in the eighteenth century. These elements helped to sustain the health of women in the childbearing age, which in turn helped improve the survival chances of infants. These conditions also increased the chances of infants surviving to adulthood since most infectious diseases have a higher incidence among youth. Therefore, the infant mortality rate must have been lower than presumed, especially during the seventeenth century when these advantages in the environment were at their peak.

Continuing Developments

Much of the information which challenges a number of the traditional expectations concerning the colonial family is the result of relatively recent studies. These studies are an important step in developing the most accurate description possible of the colonial family system. However, the scope of these works is limited and further efforts are required. As Greven (1967:443) has observed, the fullest development of "early American history... cannot focus exclusively upon the accumulation of data from vital records, nor should it be mesmerized by the prospects of quantification." Sources of a qualitative nature and "verbal data" are essential to add the necessary dimensions to further inquiries concerning the family and communities. An example of the necessary dimensions was observed by Saveth (1969:326-327) in his discussion of Bailyn's concept and technique of "family style."

Before the last two decades, our image of the colonial family was based primarily upon the evidence from a restricted set of "verbal data." With the development of new techniques and an expanding interest, this earlier image is being revised by quantitative and documented facts. Before a complete and accurate portrayal of the colonial family can occur, a final step is necessary. This step involves the better understanding of the complex interrelationships between the patterns of demographic characteristics—family size, birth rates, geographical mobility, health conditions—and family patterns which cannot be quantified—authority pattern, sex role definitions, power relationships, etc. Dealing with the interrelationships between various demographic characteristics and their effect upon nonquantifiable family patterns, such as parental power and/or intergenerational control, Smith (1972, 1973a, 1973b) provides an excellent basis and example for further work in this direction. Once this final step is obtained, many family observers anticipate that located within the family will be "the basic determinants of historical change" (Saveth, 1969:326).

However, much work still needs to be done before this final step can ever be successfully completed. The work is necessary because of some limitations in the present status of the "restoration" of the colonial American family. These limitations also indicate the direction of further study. Although dealing with the general subject of the colonial family, the majority of data thus far reported are limited to families located in New England. Hence, it is necessary to provide data on family variables for the Middle and Southern colonies, especially in light of some substantial demographic differences that existed which might have important implications for the colonial family (cf., Potter, 1965). Differences are to be expected even among the families located in the New England colonies, and the communities which have been studied thus far do vary significantly on some aspects. Certainly different factors affected the family in a coastal settlement like Ipswich, which depended primarily upon maritime industries, than in an agricultural community like Plymouth. In addition, virtually no data are available for families residing in frontier settlements, although indications are that some major differences existed (Laslett, 1970:85-86). Further study is necessary of other factors that played a role in the family behavior of the colonial American population. Some of this work has begun, but further efforts are necessary both in relating to the more observable variables, such as migration (cf., Potter, 1965; Norton, 1971:433-436; Smith, 1972:174), landholding customs (Henretta, 1971:389-391), age distribution, sex ratio, and some of the less visible variables, such as family limitation and relative age of husband in relation to wife's fertility (Smith, 1972:180-182). What remains to be done seems almost limitless. Yet the work already completed and the growing interest in it should result in a better understanding of the colonial family and its surrounding physical and social environment.

Summary

As a result of the works surveyed, a new, more realistic image of the colonial family has emerged. In short, the colonial family appears to be structurally similar to the present family in the United States. Colonial families were predominantly restricted or were nuclear units, which, at any given point in time (cross-sectionally), were similar in size to present family units. This similarity in size is especially striking in the eighteenth century due to higher mortality and lower fertility rates as compared to those that existed in the seventeenth century. The biggest differences result when one compares the completed colonial family to the contemporary completed family. But even these differences are not as large as previously assumed. Infant mortality even in the 1700s did not play as major a role in affecting family size as has commonly been assumed. Furthermore, mounting evidence suggests that certain behavioral patterns presumed unique to the contemporary family also existed in the colonial family system (cf., Adams, 1975:58-65). There appears to be more similarities between these two family systems than differences. It is surprising, but accurate, that this is a recent perspective in the study of the family. This is primarily due to the former over-emphasis upon the phenomenon of change, which has led to a neglect of what has remained permanent in the American family structure. In support, Aries (1962:9) observed that the "historical differences [in the family] are of little importance in comparison with the huge mass of what remains unchanged." Important changes have occurred, but the focus must be upon exactly what has changed and the factors which have brought about this change.

The study of the colonial family is by no means complete; much work remains to be done. Although the emphasis in this chapter has been upon the structural similarity between the colonial and the contemporary family system, there are important differences. Changes, occurring in the patterns of premarital sexual behavior and norms, husband and wife roles and divorce laws, have been widely accepted by family observers (cf., Adams, 1975:66-78). A major difficulty is that patterns of this nature lend themselves less to quantification. This becomes even more of a problem because most of the data concerning these patterns were never recorded or can no longer be obtained. The work must continue on these patterns, however, despite the difficulties of providing a full account of what has changed and to what extent it has changed since the colonial family.

The colonial family data presented here can also be used as baselines in comparing family data from later periods. The next chapter presents structural data for the American family during the nineteenth century. Despite the abundance of data (at least it is more accessible) for this era, it has actually been studied less than the colonial America.

Chapter 3

FAMILY STRUCTURE IN
THE NINETEENTH CENTURY

Because numerous studies have focused upon colonial towns and areas, it is now possible to present a more accurate and detailed portrayal of the American colonial family. Despite this vast extension of our knowledge, the data we now have are neither totally representative nor complete. The limitations of the colonial family data must be overcome if we are to have a definitive analysis of historical change for family structure. It is necessary to have data that are accurate, detailed, and comparable on the structural aspects of the family. Such data are available for the nineteenth century as a result of the decennial census begun in the United States in 1790.

Most of the historical data available on the family have been limited to extant verbal data. Consequently, the families portrayed usually were the most wealthy, influential, and representative of ideal expectations (cf., Saveth, 1969:313-314). Any generalizations based upon this atypical segment of the American population must be extremely limited in scope. As for the colonial family, the nineteenth century did not appear to have data establishing the historical baselines necessary to determine family change. Obtaining the data necessary to correct these deficiencies has been thought to be an impossible task. Hence those families which left no written record were apparently lost in history. But this is not the case since the United States started collecting information about "family" units for the entire population with its first decennial census in 1790.

The use of census material, however, must be limited to the period from 1850 to 1880. From the 1790 census through the 1840 census, the prime concern was enumeration of the population. The unit used as a basis for most of the data collected was the household or family unit (which were usually considered synonymous). Limited information on the "family" was reported for this period. Even though copies of the original manuscript schedules are available virtually no relevant information for this study can be gained from them.

A change in the enumeration procedure, starting with the 1850 census, provided what is called the most important revision made in the history of the census (Peterson, 1969:34-35). The basic unit of collection in the 1850 census was the individual (although still grouped by dwelling residence). Each individual was listed by name with additional information recorded. This practice still continues. Not only was more information reported by the Census Bureau, but the original manuscript schedules (which are available on microfilm) provide a wealth of information that formerly was never tabulated or reported. Peterson (1969:33-34) provided a summary of this information. Most important is that the existence and availability of these schedules made possible the reconstruction of individual family units. Regrettably, this situation ends after 1880. The use of the 1890 census manuscript schedules must be limited to the reports that were issued because almost all of the original census manuscript schedules were destroyed by a fire before they were duplicated. Starting with the 1900 census, the manuscript schedules are classified as "confidential" by law. Until recently from 1900 on, the only data available were those which had been reported by the census bureau in aggregate form.

(The manuscript schedules for the 1900 census have become an exception to this. Personal correspondence with both the Bureau of the Census and the National Archives and Records Service indicates that the status of the 1900 schedules has changed. These records are now in the custody of and under the control of the National Archivist. The manuscript schedules are now on microfilm and the complete set should be available sometime in 1978.

The Use of Census Manuscript Schedules

U.S. Census manuscript schedules from 1850 to 1880 were first brought to my attention by Herman R. Lantz (Lantz and Alix, 1970), who had used them in his own research. Numerous other social scientists have either utilized (Thernstrom, 1964:241-242) or expounded upon (Lathrop, 1968:79-101) the research value of these schedules. A number of sociologists and historians are using them to study the family in specific communities (cf., Campbell, 1974:369-398; Farber, 1973; B. Laslett, 1973) or for certain ethnic groups (cf., Hershberg, 1973:6-20).

Two reasons necessitating the use of the original manuscript schedules are that not all variables to be investigated are reported in the aggregate publications, and that the definitions of the family used by the census to collect information has varied throughout the history of the census.

The census bureau's most frequently reported "family" statistic for the period from 1850 to 1880 was the number of individuals per dwelling unit. In most cases these figures were considered synonymous with family size. But the original manuscript schedules report additional information such as surname, sex, age, and so forth, whereby one can determine the various structural aspects for each family unit. (For a discussion of the relevant family information available, see Appendix C.) An additional advantage is that each family unit can be directly associated with variables that measure the processes of industrialization and urbanization. This latter advantage is pursued in the following chapter.

Because the definition of what makes up a family has varied throughout the history of the census, the statistics reported by the census bureau are not comparable over time.

Based upon the initial generalization presented in Chapter 1, family size should decrease with the development of urbanization and industrialization. Concomitant with the decrease in family size, a decrease in the number of generations living within the family unit and a decline in the number of children in each family would be expected. Table 3.1 is based upon data reported by the United States Census Bureau and lends some support to these expectations. If the mean size reported for the 1950 population is compared to the one for 1790, we find that family size has declined and that the probability of having more than two generations or more than two children in the same family unit has decreased for 1950, assuming that both parents of a procreation unit are living in the family—the modal case—only two individuals (1.54) remain to be located. If these two people are assumed to be children, only two generations are in the family of residence. If one person is a grandparent, then only one child would be in the unit. The point is that no matter what form the 3.54 persons take, the family unit is too small to construct an extended family in the traditional sense. On the other hand, the figure for 1850 (5.55) allows more flexibility in structure. Although the figures for the 1800s are not as large as some individuals might have expected, Table 3.1 clearly suports the argument of an important and linear decline in family size. In fact the figure for 1790 (5.79) is even higher than some of the averages reported for the colonial family in Chapter 2.

Upon closer examination, it becomes clear that a comparison between the means in Table 3.1 is not valid because the applied definition of family has not been constant in every census. In fact, the Census Bureau has used three different definitions for the family of which only the last is parallel to the previously discussed definition for the family of residence. Before the 1930 census, with the exception of the 1900 and 1790 censuses, the family was defined "as any group of person sharing a common abode, or a person living alone" (United States: Bureau of the Census, 1949:18). As a result, many institutions and quasi-households— boarding houses, inns, hotels, army barracks, and so forth—were counted as family units. In the censuses of 1790 and 1900, the family count was limited to private families but included any lodgers and other nonrelatives who lived in the same household as members of these private families.

Table 3.1: Families–Number and Size, 1870 to 1950
(as reported by the U.S. Bureau of the Census)[a]

Year	Number of Families	Median Size of Families	Mean Size of Family
1950	42,857,335	3.05	3.52
1940	34,948,666	3.15	3.77[b]
1930	29,904,663	3.40	4.11[b]
1920	24,351,676	–	4.34[b]
1910	20,255,555	–	4.54[b]
1900	15,963,965	4.23	4.76[b]
1890	12,690,152	4.48	4.93[b]
1880	9,945,916	–	5.04[b]
1870	7,579,363	–	5.09[b]
1860	5,210,934	–	5.28[b]
1850	3,598,240	–	5.55[b]
1790	557,889	5.43	5.79[b]

a. Initially reported as family units. More recent reports have termed these units households. Source: United States: Bureau of the Census, 1960a:16.

b. Obtained by dividing total population by number of families; hence not strictly average size of private families because total population includes an appreciable number of persons who are members of quasi-households. Source: United States: Bureau of the Census, 1949:29; and 1960a:16.

After 1930, the definition of the family was changed to include "the head of a household and all other members of the household related to the head" (Glick, 1957:210). In other words, the head of a household living alone was counted as a family, but a related group of lodgers or resident employees in a household were not considered a family unit. Criticism of this definition led to another revision in 1947: "A group of two or more persons who live together and who are related by blood, marriage, or adoption are regarded as members of one family even though they may include a 'subfamily'" (Glick, 1957:210). A subfamily is a nuclear family (not including the family head) related to at least one other individual, nuclear family, or more in a given household. Because of this transformation of the family definition, the figures in Table 3.1 refer only to the number of households, the median number of individuals in each household, and the mean number of individuals per household prior to 1930. (Some distinction was made between household units and "family" dwelling units, primarily in large urban areas. In large housing units, such as duplexes, tenements, etc., individual family dwelling units were sometimes enumerated separately. But even in these individual family dwelling units, secondary families and nonrelatives, when present, were still counted incorrectly as part of the primary family. To be consistent in the sample's count, each housing unit, even when separate family dwelling units were designated, was considered one household. The effect of this upon household statistics is discussed later when Table 3.2 and 3.3 are presented.)

The figures for 1940 in Table 3.1 did eliminate nonrelatives in the household from the primary familiy. However, two additional problems were introduced. On the one hand, when no other relatives were present and the head of the household was considered a family, the mean and median were incorrectly reduced. On the other hand, this definition did not recognize the existence of secondary families (family units in a household that are not related to its head). Secondary families, on the average, are smaller than primary families and tend to reduce both the mean and median. The omission of secondary families in 1940 led to an exaggerated mean and median. Thus, counterbalancing biases existed.

The changes in definition make it necessary to go back to the available census manuscript schedules (1850-1880) to obtain comparable data on the structural aspects of the family. The information available on these schedules means a recounting procedure can be applied to provide comparable data to that collected under the definition used by the census after 1947.

The Recounting Procedure

Except for one census, data available on the census manuscript schedules used to determine family structure, are not entirely complete. In addition, the data are sometimes inaccurate because of incorrectly recorded and incomplete responses. Despite these difficulties, a great deal of information is available that helps to determine the relationship of each member in a household to the head. Specifically, a distinction can be made between family and nonfamily members in a household and a number of structural aspects for each family unit can be detemined.

Beginning with the 1850 census, each individual habitant of a household was listed by name (including usually first name as well as family name) with additional information included. Of the information recorded, the following was utilized: name, age, sex, position in household listing, and birth place. These were used to determine an individual's family or household position. The pivotal position was household head in that all other positions—spouse, child, parent. etc.—were determined or described by their relationship to the head. The only exception was for the 1880 census, where the relationship of each household member to the head was actually reported. It was only for the 1850, 1860, and 1870 censuses that the relationships had to be inferred. Hence the 1880 schedules were used to provide a basis for establishing a recounting procedure to apply to the earlier censuses and to provide an estimate of the amount of error that occurred in the recount. In addition to the 1880 schedules, the recounting procedure utilized the experience gained in an earlier exploratory study (Seward, 1974) that used the 1850 census manuscript schedules. (For a more detailed discussion of the recounting procedure used, see Appendix C.) The first step performed in the recounting procedure was to determine the membership of the primary family (containing the household head), the membership of any coexisting secondary families, and the elimination of any nonrelatives who were resident employees or lodgers in each sample household unit. Two criteria were used to determine this breakdown. First, family or common surname was considered to indicate membership in the same family. Since the most typical family unit was nuclear in structure, the majority of households were made up only of individuals sharing the same surname—the primary family. In each of the four census years surveyed, at least 65 percent of the households contained only primary family members.

However, relying upon name alone would eliminate some relatives with different surnames. To minimize this problem, the order in which individuals were presented was taken into consideration. Based upon instructions given the census marshals for these censuses (cf., Appendix C) and the way the instructions were utilized, Wright (1900) provided a very inclusive order for listing individuals. Members of the household were usually listed as follows: household head, spouse, unmarried children of head, married children of head, grandchildren, parents and parents-in-law, other relatives, servants, boarders, etc. Previous experience and the 1880 schedules suggest that individuals were listed in this order with very few exceptions.

Although the initial decision in determining family membership was based upon common family name, any individuals having surnames different from the family head's but listed in a position indicating family membership and having the appropriate age or sex characteristics, were included as family members, e.g., a male, a female, or couple following the spouse of a male household head. If any such individuals had different surnames than the head, ages suggesting they might be parents of the head's spouse, or were followed by a number of children with the same surname as that of the head, they were included as family members. In the listing order, separating or determining "other" relatives proved to be difficult. For individuals in this position, common surname was the determining criterion. Data presented later will confirm this as a problematical area.

Once family membership for both primary and secondary units was established the next step was to determine several structural aspects of the family. To do this, the relationships between the family members had to be established. Using essentially the same information as above, that is, age, sex, position in family listing, and sometimes birth place, the family positions were ascertained. The value ranges of the characteristics used to determine an individual's family position are presented in Table C.1 in Appendix C. The criteria applied (the value ranges) were adequate to cover most situations and positions; however, a limited number of cases were found for which the procedure did not apply or for which information was incomplete. In these cases, individual decisions were based upon what information was available, past experience, and what seemed to be appropriate. Finally, those household members who were not a part of any family unit were categorized either as resident employees (if they listed an occupation) or lodgers.

Once the recounting procedure was established, it was applied to a sample of households recorded on the original manuscript census schedules from the 1850, 1860, 1870, and 1880 censuses.

A National Sample of Households*

Individual selection of families from all the available individual manuscript census schedules for the U.S. population from 1850 to 1880 would be too expensive and nearly impossible. To facilitate the selection of a sample and, at the same time, provide a representative sample, a stratified cluster sampling procedure was used. The states (29) that were a part of the United States as of January 1850 constituted the geographical boundaries of the area from which the sample of households was drawn.

The first step in the sampling procedure was to place all of the states into one of three strata—Northeast, North Central (Midwest), and South. (For the list of states by strata and a more detailed discussion of the sampling procedure, see Appendix B.) A number of considerations led to this stratification. First, the state strata represent different geographical regions in the United States. Also, to allow comparisons to data from later censuses, the state strata were based upon the same regional divisons used by the United States Census Bureau (1960a: xii, 16, 18, 20, 25) during the twentieth century. Furthermore the state strata are domains of the study in that separate data from each stratum yields additional information. This is possible because of differences in population, population growth, and economies between the strata.

Within each stratum a cluster of four states was selected through the use of a random number table. Before selection each state was weighted according to the size of its population within the strata to assure that people in the less populated states

---

*The selection, collection, and preparation of data for the nineteenth century sample of households was supported in part by a grant, GS-33863, from the National Science Foundation.

within each stratum would not be overrepresented in the cluster of selected states. After the twelve states (primary sampling units) were selected, the next step was to select from each state the secondary sampling units which were counties or their equivalent. From each state one county was selected from a stratum containing the state's most populated counties and one county was selected from a stratum of the state's lesser populated counties. Within each stratum each county was weighted according to its population size, and one county was selected randomly.

After the twenty-four counties (secondary sampling units) were selected, the final step was to obtain the family units or primary selections. Using a systematic sampling procedure one hundred dwelling units were chosen from each of the twenty-four counties. Then, in each of the selected sample dwelling units, the family unit or units were determined and measured for the structural aspects of the family and other characteristics studied.

A very practical consideration in selecting county units was that the microfilm on which the original manuscript census schedules were recorded are organized by counties within each state. For most of the smaller counties their complete set of census schedules are available on one microfilm roll. The use of counties offered great savings in time and cost. In addition, each county is much more homogeneous in its economic and social characteristics than are regions and states. This is particularly useful for an analysis of the processes of industrialization and urbanization (see the next chapter).

Family Structure

From the recount of the 1850 to 1880 sample the size of every household was recorded. Then for each family unit in a household the size, generational composition, number of marital pairs, and number of children for the head of the family was recorded. For at least 65 percent of the sample the household's membership was the same as its primary family membership. The remaining households were broken down into the primary family unit, any secondary family units when present, and individuals not linked

Table 3.2: Number of Households and Percentage Distribution
by Size: 1850-1880 Sample

Size of Household	1850	1860	1870	1880
All units	2,396	2,402	2,400	2.399
Percentage	100.0	100.0	100.0	100.0
1 person	2.5	2.5	2.7	3.0
2 persons	8.5	8.7	10.9	10.1
3 persons	13.6	12.7	14.4	14.7
4 persons	13.8	15.1	16.5	15.3
5 persons	13.0	15.0	15.4	15.2
6 persons	13.2	13.4	12.7	12.8
7 persons	9.8	10.6	8.4	10.5
8 persons	8.4	7.8	6.7	7.1
9 persons	5.9	5.1	4.2	4.5
10 persons	4.3	3.6	2.8	2.8
11 persons or more	6.8	5.5	5.2	3.8
Modal size	4.00	4.00	4.00	4.00
Median size	5.40	5.23	4.84	4.96
Mean size	5.83	5.68	5.40	5.33

Source: United States: Bureau of the Census, Seventh Census Population Schedules, Eighth Census Population Schedules, Ninth Census Population Schedules, and Tenth Census Population Schedules, Microfilm Publication Numbers M704, M653, M593, and T9. Washington, D.C.: National Archives and Records Service. (For rolls used, see references.)

to any family unit. The data presented below are the result of the recounting procedure.

HOUSEHOLD SIZE

Table 3.2 presents the number of sample households, their percentage distribution by size, and measures of central tendency for each census year surveyed. An overall small and steady decline in size appears to occur throughout the sample period. The reduction in size appears to be primarily due to the disappearance of large households. The distribution shows that the biggest percentage change is in the eleven persons or more category. These figures are also in line with the figures reported in Table 3.1 which show the same pace of steady decline.

The figures presented in Table 3.1 supposedly represent household size, but they are consistently around three tenths of one person smaller than the figures in Table 3.2. Since the sample is supposed to be nationally representative, these differences must be explained. The basic reason for these differences is that the recount attempts to adhere to the initial instructions given to the census marshals taking the censuses that are a part of the sample. Although the wording varied slightly for each census, the instructions were basically the same. Each dwelling house or household referred to "a house standing alone, or separated by walls from other houses in a block" (Wright, 1900:156). These households could contain one or more "families" as long as they were all under the same roof. While some dwelling houses (households) were divided into "families," such public units as "hotels, poorhouses, garrisons, hospitals, asylums, jails, penitentiaries, and other similar institutions" (p. 151) were considered one household.

A "family," which in most cases was synonymous with its household unit in terms of membership, could consist of

> one person living separately in a house or a part of a house, and providing for him or herself, or several persons living together in a house, or in part of a house [depending] upon one common means of support. . . . [Thus] a widow living alone and separately providing for herself, or 200 individuals living together and provided for by a common head, should each be numbered as one family (p. 151).

Also, the inmates of the public institutions listed above (hotels, etc.) were considered one family with the landlord, jailor, etc. considered the head of the family. As a result there were two household size figures for each census from 1850 to 1880. The figures in Table 3.1 are based upon the membership of dwelling houses where only one "family" unit was designated, plus membership for each "family" unit when a dwelling house was subdivided into "family" dwelling units. (But because of the definitions applied, this is still an incorrect figure. This would be true even if we only dealt with those "families" that resulted from a subdivision of larger dwelling houses. The reason is that in both instances the "family's" membership was determined only

Table 3.3: Mean Household Size for Sample Versus Mean Dwelling
House Size as Reported by Census, 1850-1880

Census Year	Sample	Census Figure
1850	5.83	5.94
1860	5.68	5.53
1870	5.40	5.47
1880	5.33	5.60

Source: Table 3.2 and United States: Bureau of the Census, 1883a:669.

by the fact that they lived separately and/or shared the same
table and not by any discrimination based on blood, marriage,
or adoption ties.)

In the recount used in this study the household size recorded
was equivalent to the dwelling houses' memberships as designated by the census marshals. Any subdivision into family
dwelling units was ignored. Hence, the figures in Table 3.1 should
be smaller. This, then, explains the higher household figures
for the sample. To further support this claim the sample household means are compared in Table 3.3 to the means reported by
the census bureau for dwelling house units. These means are
much closer to one another and would lend support to the
sample's representativeness. The sample figures do tend to be
smaller than those reported by the census, with the exception
of the 1860 figures. A practical explanation for this was the
omission of poorhouses, jails, and other public dwelling houses
from the sample which would make the application of the recount
procedure extremely difficult and much more tentative. However, small inns, boarding houses, and hotels were included in
the sample.

Hence, as expected, a steady decline in household size occurred
during the sample period as a result of a reduction in the number
of large households. Under the definitions applied at the time of
the census, the sample household size figures would have represented "family" size (although adhering strictly to the procedure
would mean some reduction in these figures). If presented as
family size figures (as the Table 3.1 figures in fact were), the indication would be a reduction in family size by almost one half when

compared to contemporary figures. This would lend support to the traditional perspective. The next concern is the size figures for only those individuals who were members of the same family and who shared the same household.

FAMILY SIZE

The recounting procedure provided for the measurement of family units that consisted only of individuals related by blood, marriage, or adoption who shared the dwelling unit. Table 3.4 presents the results of the recount and provides the measures relating to the size of the family of residence based upon the information recorded on the manuscript schedules by the census marshals for each census year in the sample. The family units used to compile these data included all the primary and secondary family units found in the sample households. This is true for all tables in this study that present family statistics unless otherwise stated. As subfamilies are only considered one possible component of a family unit, they were not considered separate family units in compiling these data.

The recount results in reductions for each census year for the family size figures initially reported by the census and for household sizes reported in Table 3.2.

The differences between the initially reported "family" means (Table 3.1) and the sample family means (Table 3.4) are .76 for 1850, .59 for 1860, .69 for 1870, and .21 for 1880. The differences are understated, however, as one person "families" were included in the calculation of the means in Table 3.1. Based upon a recalculation for those figures available it is estimated that the elimination of one person "families" would increase the means in Table 3.1 and result in a difference of about two-tenths of a person for each census year (cf., United States: Bureau of the Census, 1866:315).

The reduction from sample household size figures (Table 3.2) are around one person for 1850, 1860, and 1870 and only a half a person for 1880. This suggests that the steady decline observed for household size does not occur for family size. A steady decline occurs from 1850 to 1870 but the figure for 1880 increases and is, in fact, a bit higher than the figure reported for 1850.

Table 3.4: Number of Families and Percentage Distribution
by Size, 1850-1880 Sample

Size of Family	1850	1860	1870	1880
All units	2,684	2,666	2,712	2,496
Percentage	100.0	100.0	100.0	100.0
2 persons	18.5	17.9	21.8	15.7
3 persons	18.6	17.2	19.5	17.1
4 persons	16.2	17.3	18.5	17.3
5 persons	12.9	16.2	13.8	15.6
6 persons	11.2	11.3	9.8	12.1
7 persons	7.8	8.4	6.7	9.1
8 persons	6.4	5.4	4.6	6.4
9 persons	3.7	3.3	2.4	3.2
10 persons	2.5	1.8	1.4	2.0
11 persons or more	2.1	1.2	1.4	1.4
Modal size	3.00	2.00	2.00	4.00
Median size	4.30	4.35	3.97	4.49
Mean size	4.79	4.69	4.40	4.83

Source: United States: Bureau of the Census, Seventh Census Population Schedules, Eighth Census
Population Schedules, Ninth Census Population Schedules, and Tenth Census Population Schedules,
Microfilm Publication Numbers M704, M653, M593, and T9. Washington, D.C.: National Archives
and Records Service. (For rolls used, see references.)

Despite the shift in means the majority of families for each year
surveyed were composed of four members or less. The lowest
percentage was for 1880, where only 50.2 percent of the family
units had four or less persons; the highest percentage was for
1870 with 59.9 percent, while 1850 (53.3) and 1860 (52.3) were
nearer the 1880 figure. Also, over 65 percent of the families in
each year's sample were in units of five persons or less. With a
dominant family size of four or smaller, it is impossible for the
ideal extended type of family, expected to predominate in this
time period, to exist in any significant numbers (Burch, 1970;
Wozniak, 1972:10). The rest of the data adds further support to
this proposition.

The traditional perspective of changing family structure would
suggest a much larger discrepancy between family sizes than that
shown in the sample and contemporary figures. Using the mean
(3.57) and median (3.20) reported by the U.S. Bureau of the
Census (1973: 23 and 55) for 1970, the difference ranges from

less than one individual per family (a mean difference of .83 and median difference of .77 for 1870) to a little over one individual per family (a mean difference of 1.26 and a median difference of 1.29 for 1880). These differences are certainly much less than the earlier contentions anticipated.

Another consideration must be the reversal of the downward trend for family size in 1880. This increase in family size is of particular interest as this was the only census where all household residents were identified on the manuscript census schedule by their relationship to the household head. Hence, it is possible that the lower figures for 1850 to 1870 result primarily from the elimination of household members who were, in fact, family members. One test of this is to compare the family structural statistics for all sample families (both primary and secondary) to a subgroup of families for whom bias through the recount was highly unlikely. Such a subgroup existed and was composed of those family units whose membership equaled the membership of the household in which the family resided. In other words, these households contained only one primary family unit. With very few exceptions all the individuals in these primary family households shared the same surname. No secondary families or nonrelatives were determined or even suspected of being present. Hence, the possibility of bias was not introduced by the elimination of nonfamily members. Over 60 percent of the households for each sample year consisted only of a primary family unit. Table 3.5 presents the number, distribution, and measures of central tendency for these primary family households.

The data overall suggest a similar trend for both samples. The mean and median gradually decline from 1850 to 1870 and both increased in 1880. In the percentage distributions, the major difference is for two person families. However, this is expected because secondary families, who are included in Table 3.4, have a much smaller average size. In fact, a high proportion of secondary families in the sample were either young married couples or a single adult parent with one or more children. Hence the increase in 1880 family size apparently did not result from the recounting procedure. As the other structural aspects of the family are presented, the statistics for these primary family household

Table 3.5: Number of Primary Families when Membership Equal to Household Size, and Percentage Distribution by Size: 1850-1880 Sample

Size of Family	1850	1860	1870	1880
All units	1,561	1,556	1,591	1,813
Percentage	100.0	100.0	100.0	100.0
2 persons	11.9	12.3	15.2	13.0
3 persons	17.1	15.6	18.2	16.7
4 persons	16.1	18.3	18.9	16.8
5 persons	13.3	16.3	15.8	15.3
6 persons	12.8	12.7	11.4	12.7
7 persons	9.4	10.2	7.7	10.2
8 persons	7.8	6.8	5.8	7.4
9 persons	4.9	3.9	3.1	3.8
10 persons	3.4	2.3	1.9	2.4
11 persons or more	3.4	1.5	1.9	1.7
Modal size	3.00	4.00	4.00	4.00
Median size	4.87	4.74	4.38	4.73
Mean size	5.28	5.05	4.78	5.04

Source: United States: Bureau of the Census, Seventh Census Population Schedules, Eighth Census Population Schedules, Ninth Census Population Schedules, and Tenth Census Population Schedules, Microfilm Publication Numbers M704, M653, M593, and T9. Washington, D.C.: National Archives and Records Service. (For rolls used, see references.)

units are also presented (usually in parenthesis) for comparison and as checks upon the effects of the recounting procedure.

These comparisons also question the advisability of basing rules for inferring household and family relationships upon data presented in the 1880 manuscript census schedules as done by Miller (1972). It will become more and more apparent that the 1880 data appear to represent a reversal of many earlier trends in regard to family structure.

The data suggest that family size for the sample period has not been much larger than contemporary figures and has, at the same time, been smaller than those family size figures originally reported by the census. Finally, an apparent decline in family size occurred from 1850 to 1870 followed by a fairly sharp rise in size for 1880. The structural elements that account for smaller than expected sizes and for this increase in size in 1880 become clear as the other structural aspects of the family are observed.

Table 3.6: Families by Generational Composition:
Percentage Restricted versus Extended for 1850-1880 Sample

Year	Percentage	Restricted (one or two generations)	Extended (three or more generations)
1850	100.0	97.6 (97.5)[a]	2.4 (2.5)[a]
1860	100.0	97.3 (97.4)	2.7 (2.6)
1870	100.0	96.6 (95.7)	3.4 (4.3)
1880	100.0	92.6 (92.4)	7.3 (7.6)

Source: Same as Table 3.2.
   a. Based upon the subsample of primary family households where the only residents of the household are primary family members.

GENERATIONAL COMPOSITION

A fundamental question about family structural change involves the frequency of extended families present during the sample period. For the sample families, both vertical extension (more than two generations in a family) and horizontal extension (more than two marital pairs in the same generation) were recorded when present. Table 3.6 presents the percentage of restricted and vertically extended families for each sample year. Only a small percentage of the sample families exhibited vertical extension; the highest percentage was in 1880, a figure of only 7.3. Although only a small number of families were extended, the proportion did consistently increase from 1850 to 1880 with the biggest jump occurring between 1870 and 1880. Again, as a check on the recount in parenthesis the data for the subsample of primary family households (households that contain only a primary family and no nonrelatives of the household head) are presented. For this group the trend and the percentages are very similar to those for all families. As a further check on the recount, all those family members in the 1880 sample with a surname different from the family head's and who added a generation to the family were eliminated. *Some* of these individuals in the earlier censuses would probably have been considered lodgers, depending on their location in the household list (see Appendix C). When *all* of these individuals are eliminated, the percentage of extended families is reduced to 4.2

percent; however, this figure is still higher than any of the figures reported for all family units for 1850 to 1870. Hence the trend toward an increasing proportion of extended families during the sample period is supported.

It is interesting that most of the figures presented for the sample years are lower than those reported for the twentieth century. In fact, only the 1880 figure appears to surpass the contemporary figures (5.5 for 1960; 7.2 for 1970) reported by the U.S. Bureau of the Census (1963a:450; 1973:207). Two factors that help explain this difference are a decreasing rate of geographical mobility and an increase in immigrant families throughout the sample period (see Table 3.13). The latter is explored later in this chapter.

Horizontal extension was almost completely absent during the sample period. Less than three-tenths of one percent of the sample families contained more than one marital pair in the same generation. Apparently, a family unit with two siblings and their families of procreation in the same household was virtually non-existent. As the evidence suggests, the other relatives in the family unit (those outside of the nuclear family containing the head) either tended to add a generation (parents or grandchildren of the head) or, if these "others" were of the same generation, they tended to be unmarried siblings or siblings who had children and an absent spouse.

Sometimes individuals who were not a part of a nuclear family containing a family head did form separate nuclear families or subfamilies. This occurred even less than vertical extension, as Table 3.7 indicates. The trends are much the same as in Table 3.6, with only a very small percent of the sample families having a subfamily residing under the same roof. Again, the figures for the subsample of primary family households show much the same trend and percentages. As a further check, all subfamilies in 1880 having a different surname than the family head were eliminated. The resulting percentage was 2.5. This figure is lower than the 1870 figure and only a little larger than the 1860 figure. The 2.5 figure suggests less of an increase than the other two sets of figures in Table 3.7, but nonetheless this figure is larger than the ones reported for the first two censuses. This figure also

Table 3.7: Percentage of Families with and without Subfamilies:
1850-1880 Sample

Year	Total	No Subfamilies	One Subfamily or More
1850	100.0	98.1 (98)[a]	01.9 (2.0)[a]
1860	100.0	97. (97.6)	02.3 (2.4)
1870	100.0	97.0 (96.5)	03.0 (03.5)
1880	100.0	96.0 (96.0)	04.0 (04.0)

Source: Same as Table 3.2.
  a. Based upon a subsample of primary family households where the only resident of the household are primary family members.

suggests (as the others do) that little variance in the percent of families with subfamilies occurred during the sample period.

It must however be kept in mind that not all of these sub-families with different surnames would have been eliminated in the earlier censuses (1850 to 1870). This fact added to the figures reported for those families in the sample and subsample having subfamilies indicates a slight increase in this phenomenon. Hence some of the increase in family size for 1880 might be related to this slight rise in the existence of subfamilies and to an even larger increase in the number of other relatives who genera-tionally extended the family. It is also suggested later that there might have been some tendency to replace secondary families with subfamilies. A related concern is that the location of some subfamilies in the household listing with surnames different from the head's meant that the chances of inferring that they were subfamilies and not secondary families were, in fact, reduced.

Although some questions about the accuracy of the recount can be raised, especially in the area of subfamilies, the overall picture cannot be forgotten. Over 90 percent of the families in the sample were restricted or nuclear units with only one nuclear family present in each household. Also, the increase in the size of families for 1880 is explained to some small degree by the rise in extended families and the presence of more subfamilies, with the latter being less important and less reliable.

Finally, the general trend for extended families and families with a subfamily is different than that for family size data. While size decreased gradually from 1850 to 1870, a gradual increase occurred in the number of extended families and families with subfamilies throughout the sample period. These trends are in line with a phenomenon observed in other census data (Burch, 1967:363) from a different period. This phenomenon can be defined as the tendency for family members outside of the head's nuclear family to be present in the absence of the head's own spouse and/or children rather than in addition to these family members. For some reason this relationship breaks down for 1880 as almost all of the family structural variables that would add to family size show an increase.

MARITAL PAIRS

Table 3.8 presents the number of marital pairs per family for each sample year. The number of marital pairs per family have varied very little throughout the sample period and are very similar to the figures reported for contemporary data—for 1970 the figure was .87 (United States: Bureau of the Census, 1973:23, 225). Again, contrary to expectation, the lowest figures are reported for the sample period and even the highest figure for 1880 is lower than the figure reported for 1960 by two hundredths of a point. For the primary family households the trends are fairly similar but even less variation occurs. As a further check all the marital pairs for 1880 with a different surname than the family's head were considered part of secondary family units. But, the resulting figure (.87) was still higher than the earlier censuses figures for all families. Again these checks support the accuracy of the recount.

This aspect displays much less variation than was the case for families with subfamilies and for extended families. Hence, the addition of married pairs to the family played only a very small role in the increase in family size for 1880 as the lack of horizontal extension also suggests.

A different trend than for the other structural aspects is occurring here. The figure declines in 1860 from a higher figure for 1850, then increases for 1870, and increases again for 1880, which is the highest figure for any sample year. Hence a reversal of an expected decreasing trend occurs.

Table 3.8: Number of Marital Pairs per Family: 1850-1880 Sample

Year	Families	Number of Marital Pairs	Number of Marital Pairs per Family
1850	2,684 (1,561)[a]	2,272 (1,396)[a]	.85 (.89)[a]
1860	2,666 (1,556)	2,216 (1,360)	.83 (.87)
1870	2,712 (1,591)	2,270 (1,410)	.84 (.89)
1880	2,496 (1,813)	2,202 (1,635)	.88 (.90)

Source: Same as Table 3.2.
   a. Based upon subsample of primary family households.

A related aspect is the percent of families who have both the head and his spouse present in the family (see Table 3.9). The vast majority of families (over 80 percent contain a marital pair which includes the family head and his spouse. The trend is similar to the one for the number of marital pairs—the figure first declining to the lowest level in 1860 and then increasing for the following two censuses. These figures are very similar to those reported for the twentieth century, although the nineteenth century figures tend to be a bit lower. This means that in the nineteenth century the chances were slightly less of having a family headed by a married couple. This is important because these figures, i.e., the percentage of families headed by a marital pair, have been used to indicate family stability (Farley and Hermalin, 1971:5-7). However, due to such factors as differences in head-spouse mortality, percentage of population married, divorce rates, etc., the percentage of families headed by single individuals (family instability) has remained essentially the same for both periods.

As a check the figures from the subsample of primary family households are presented in parentheses. These data follow the same trend as the one for all families, but the figures for families headed by a marital pair are somewhat higher. This is expected since secondary families tended to have a much higher percentage of families headed by single individuals.

To some degree these figures add support to a phenomenon mentioned earlier, that is, the tendency for "other" family relatives to be present in the absence of the family head's spouse or

Table 3.9: Percentage of Families by Presence of Head and Spouse
or Head only: 1850-1880 Sample

Year	Percentage	Head-Spouse Families	Head only
1850	100.0	83.4 (88.3)[a]	16.7 (11.7)[a]
1860	100.0	81.4 (85.5)	18.6 (14.5)
1870	100.0	82.1 (87.0)	17.9 (13.0)
1880	100.0	85.5 (87.5)	14.4 (12.5)

Source: Same as Table 3.2.
   a. Based upon a subsample of primary family households.

children. For the first three censuses an overall decrease in the percentage of families headed by a marital couple occurs while the number of extended families and families with subfamilies increases. In 1880 this breaks down as the highest figure for head-spouse families coincides with an increase in these other aspects as well as in family size.

A related statistic, which has also been used to indicate family instability (p. 6), is the sex of the family's head. An increasing proportion of families headed by females has been taken to indicate instability because this type of single parent family usually results from divorce, death, desertion, etc. This is true because, regardless of the actual circumstances, the male has almost automatically been considered the head by the census marshal when both the head and a spouse are present. Based upon the traditional perspective regarding family structural change (a patriarchal authority pattern) one might expect a lower percentage of families headed by females in the nineteenth century; but the data presented in Table 3.10 do not support this contention. First of all, the percentage of female-headed families (as well as male-headed) is very similar throughout the sample period, and very similar to the contemporary figures. The only figure that is lower than the 1950 to 1970 figures is the 1850 figure (8.9) and this is only four tenths of one percent lower. Although these are only small increases, the trend is one of a rising percentage of female-headed families from 1850 to 1870 with a return in 1880 to the 1860 figure. Hence, the percentage of couple-headed families during the sample period have re-

Table 3.10: Sex of Family Head by Percentage: 1850-1880 Sample

Year	Families	Percentage Male Head	Percentage Female Head
1850	2,684 (1,561)[a]	91.1 (93.9)[a]	8.9 (6.1)[a]
1860	2,666 (1,556)	89.8 (91.9)	10.1 (8.1)
1870	2,712 (1,591)	88.9 (91.5)	11.1 (8.5)
1880	2,496 (1,813)	89.8 (91.1)	10.1 (8.9)

Source: Same as Table 3.2.
  a. Based upon a subsample of primary family households.

mained remarkably stable, which suggests (assuming this is at least one measure of it) family stability. The pattern of designating the eldest male child, married or unmarried, as the head in families where only the mother resided in the household did not emerge as would be expected under a more traditional patriarchal family system. In fact, many instances occurred where women were designated as family heads without any occupation or property value listed (which if listed might indicate or be supportive of head status) even though they were followed by a son who had an occupation or property value listed.

Again, the figures in parentheses from Table 3.10, which indicate primary family households, show a fairly identical trend to the one for all families with a slight alteration—the 1880 figure for males continues to decline, although only slightly, instead of rising.

The data relating to the marital pairs, the head's marital status, and the head's sex seem to suggest that few changes took place in these aspects in the later half of the nineteenth century. Apparently, the incidence of these aspects was very similar to that exhibited today.

NUMBER OF CHILDREN

The final structural aspect of the family dealt with is the number of children per family. Table 3.11 presents the number, percent distribution, and measures of central tendency for the children of each family head. For each of the sample years the average number of children per family was less than three. Over 50 percent of the family units in each census year had two or less

Table 3.11: Number and Percentage Distribution of Head's Own
Children per Family: 1850-1880 Sample

Number of Children	1850	1860	1870	1880
All units	2,684 (1,561)[a]	2,666 (1,556)[a]	2,712 (1,591)[a]	2,496(1,813)[a]
Percentage	100.0	100.0	100.0	100.0
No children	18.9 (12.0)	18.3 (12.8)	21.3 (16.2)	15.9 (13.5)
1 child	19.0 (17.4)	17.5 (16.0)	21.5 (20.2)	19.4 (18.6)
2 children	16.0 (15.2)	17.5 (17.7)	17.8 (17.6)	17.2 (16.8)
3 children	13.0 (14.9)	15.0 (15.2)	14.3 (15.7)	16.2 (16.3)
4 children	11.0 (12.1)	11.9 (14.2)	9.3 (10.7)	10.9 (11.1)
5 children	7.9 (9.4)	8.4 (9.6)	6.9 (7.8)	9.1 (10.3)
6 children	5.9 (7.1)	5.2 (6.8)	4.2 (5.3)	5.4 (6.3)
7 children	4.0 (5.2)	3.3 (3.8)	2.2 (2.9)	2.9 (3.4)
8 children or more	4.6 (3.2)	2.9 (4.0)	2.6 (3.6)	2.9 (3.6)
Modal number	1.00 (1.00)	0.00 (2.00)	1.00 (1.00)	1.00 (1.00)
Median number	2.26 (2.86)	2.31 (2.73)	1.91 (2.27)	2.35 (2.57)
Mean number	2.76 (3.25)	2.67 (3.03)	2.34 (2.67)	2.70 (2.90)

Source: Same as Table 3.2.
   a. Based upon subsample of primary family households.

children. These figures are lower than expected and are not much
higher than the figures for contemporary families.

The distributions for each sample year appear generally similar
but some changes should be noted. With the exception of those
families with no children and those with one child, each category
varies around three percent throughout the sample period. The
number of families with no children exhibits the most change
(5.4 percent), and follows a seesaw pattern. The percent of families
with no children first decreases slightly, then rises abruptly to
the highest percentage in 1870, and drops off rather sharply for
1880. (For the primary family households the trend is somewhat
similar with the biggest difference being a smaller decline between 1870 and 1880.) Factors important to this pattern seem to
be the effects of the Civil War upon the family life cycle and
the first enumeration of former black slaves by household and
family units. Because of the war many children left home at an
earlier age than usual. Many were never to return and for those
who survived many moved on to other areas. Also, many families
were broken up and, as a result, many more cases of siblings

(adults in many cases) and single parent families were found residing in other families' households in 1870.

The 1870 census had the highest percentage of secondary families for any of the sample years. In that census the highest percentage of female-headed households and the next highest percentage of families headed by a single person were recorded. Among black families this seemed to be somewhat more common as a result of the existence of single parent families or adult siblings unrelated to the household head who were designated as secondary families. Even though the 1870 figures display the largest variation during the sample period, these figures are not dissimilar to those from the other sample years. The different pattern noted for some black families in 1870 should not be overemphasized because the vast majority of black families followed the same general pattern established by the general population. Other research on black families and several ethnic groups during the nineteenth century confirm that only minor variation in family structure occurred among these groups (Furstenberg et al., 1973).

The second most changing category is families with one child (4 percent). Although changing less, the same seesaw pattern as occurred in the no-children category is exhibited in this one. The highest percentage is reached in 1870 and is followed by a decline, although not as drastic as in the no-children category. Again, the Civil War probably played a role in reducing the age at which children left home, assuring that some never returned, providing opportunities outside of the family for those that survived, and breaking up families in various ways, thereby reducing family size and the number of children per family. In addition, a distinct drop in the birth rate occurred for whites during the Civil War as estimated by Coale and Zelnik (1963:21-24).

The rest of the distributions generally suggest an overall reduction of families with larger numbers of children (six or more) and an increase in the families with smaller numbers of children.

Most contemporary census statistics dealing with children per family include only those children under eighteen years of age who reside in the household. If all children of the head are included, regardless of age, the mean is usually increased by about two tenths of a person.

No age distinction was made in the sample; therefore, contemporary statistics which do not make an age distinction are used for the purpose of comparison. The largest number of children per family was recorded for 1850 and, if the mean and median for 1850 is compared to the mean (1.54) and median (1.19) for 1970 (United States: Bureau of the Census, 1963a:21), the difference is a little over one child per family. In fact, the difference for each statistic is exactly the same—1.16. Comparing the smallest figures reported for 1870 to the 1970 figures, the difference is less than one child per family—a mean difference of .80 and a median difference of .72. Again, the differences are much less than might have been expected between these two periods. These differences are almost identical to the differences found in earlier comparisons of family size. In fact, the differences between the figures for 1970 and the sample's figures for the number of children per family are, on the average, within one tenth of a person to the family size differences. In light of the relative lack of change in the other structural aspects, the decline in family size would appear to be primarily due to a reduction in the number of children per family. Hence the decline of the fertility rate (cf., Coale and Zelnik, 1963:21-27) appears to be a major factor in the decline of these two family structural aspects that have shown the most change—family size and the number of children per family. But other factors must be considered as well when observing these differences.

Since the only children included in these counts are those residing in the household at the time of enumeration, other patterns in addition to fertility are important, such as child-spacing, family life cycle, emancipation of children, and enumeration of college students. Over the last century a decrease in the average spacing interval between children has occurred along with an increasing tendency for a married couple to have all their children soon after marriage (cf., Glick, 1957:53-60; Glick and Parke, 1965:187-193). Even in the contemporary period when the number of children per woman has increased, the length of the childbearing period has not lengthened due to the decrease in spacing. As a result of this trend, the number of years that a couple will have children residing in their home has been reduced. Reducing this period even more is a decrease in the number of years children usually live with their parents. An increasing emphasis has been placed upon the emancipation of children (although not necessarily financial). One result is that a growing proportion of young people achieve a form of residential independence through college attendance. This trend is probably more dramatic for females as there has been traditionally a stronger tendency for daughters to remain in the home of their parents until marriage (Glick, 1957:67-68).

For parents these trends have meant an increasing period of joint survival after their children leave home (Glick and Parke, 1965:194-196). This means that today there is a greater probability of finding many more couples (parents) who have no children residing in their homes due to a shorter child rearing period, an earlier emancipation of children, and an extended life span of the parents. Hence, a higher percentage of those families having no children in the contemporay figures are, in fact, couples who have already discharged their child rearing responsibilities. The contemporary figures do not necessarily reflect the total number of children born per family and this fact, to some degree, increases the differences between these two periods. The percentage of couples who are childless must also be considered. The fact that the percentage of families with no children almost doubles for the contemporary census data as compared to the sample data might suggest an increase in childless couples for the later censuses. But the percentage of childless couples has formed a curvilinear pattern over the last century with the highest percentages occurring between 1890 and 1940. The percentages of childless couples for the 1850 to 1880 and 1950 to 1970 periods are fairly similar—around 8 to 10 percent (Glick and Parke, 1965:193; Peterson, 1969:507-509). Hence the trends in the family life cycle seem more important in affecting the number of couples without children recorded by the census.

Varying practices in the enumeration of children have also increased the mean and median differences between the sample period and the contemporary data. In the sample years students (and even some apprentices) who were boarding in a place away from their parents household were still listed and counted with their parental families. On the other hand college students for the 1950 to 1970 censuses were enumerated at their college residences (Parke, 1969:4). Hence, for a variety of reasons the differences for the average number of children per family of residence between the two periods are overstated.

In addition to the similar differences when the sample data are compared to contemporary data for both family size and the number of children per family, the trend for the latter (Table 3.11) is exactly the same as that for the former, with a declining mean occurring from 1850 to 1870 followed by an increase for 1880. As before, the statistics in parentheses for the primary family households subsample show much the same distribution and trends. Again this lends support to the accuracy of the recount. This also supports the belief that a close association between changes in the number of children per family and changes in total family size exists.

The Sample's Accuracy: A Final Word

A concern throughout this chapter has been the accuracy of the recount procedure. The basic check utilized up to this point has been the statistics derived from a subsample of primary family households from each sample year. These statistics tend to support the findings and the accuracy of the recount for two reasons. First, the distributions and trends for the subsample are usually fairly similar to and go in the same direction as the total sample of families. Second, the differences that do exist between the subsample and the total sample, whether for means or percentages, occur in the expected direction—the subsample families should be larger, have more children, be headed by a marital pair more often, etc.

Furthermore, additional information is available that can indicate more about the accuracy of the recount procedure. As mentioned earlier, in the 1880 census the relationship of every person to the household head was recorded. Since common

surname was the basic criterion for determining family membership in the recount for the other censuses, it is useful to note the
existence and relationships of family members having different
surnames than the family head in 1880. First of all, only 261
families out of the 2,496 total for 1880 contained a family member who had a different surname from that of the family head.
Just over 10 percent of the sample had one or more such individuals. This suggests that using family surname as a criterion
of family membership is going to be correct in the vast majority
of cases. For the majority (60 percent) of families in 1880 who
had one or more relatives who did not share the family head's
surname, only one such individual was present. As a result, few
families with such individuals contained marital pairs (10 percent) or subfamilies (14 percent) composed of family members
with different surnames. Horizontal extension of the family
resulting from the inclusion of these individuals was extremely
rare. Some or most of these subfamilies, depending on their
location in the household's listing as recorded on the census
manuscript schedules, might have been considered secondary
families if the recount procedure used for the earlier censuses
had been applied to the 1880 census and had ignored the relationships listed. Doing this affects only a small proportion of the
sample as only one percent (1.4) of the total number of families
for 1880 contained a subfamily composed of individuals having a
different surname from that of the family head. Similarly, this
suggests that for the other censuses only a very small proportion
of the total number of families would be affected. It also suggests
that during the sample period, a patrilocal residence pattern was
more frequently followed than a matrilocal one. This tendency
to follow a patrilocal pattern adds credibility to the recount
because subfamilies following a patrilocal pattern would have the
same surname as the family head.

  The most important addition made by these individuals with a
different family name was to add a generation to the family.
Although less than a majority of the families (261) contained
these individuals, a generation was added to the family in 47
percent of the cases. This then involved a higher proportion of
the total sample of families (5 percent for 1880) than did sub-

families. Although still a small proportion, this would suggest that in the recount errors in determining the relationships of these individuals, especially those not part of a subfamily, are much greater. Many of these individuals, however, were parents of head's spouse (usually only one was present) and were frequently listed after the spouse but before the head and spouse's children. Although this violates the expected order of listing (see Appendix C) it was, in fact, a common exception noted in this study's recount as well as by other researchers (cf., Miller, 1972:27-28). Adding the criteria of listing order to common surname should have reduced the amount of error in determining the relationships of family members with different family names who added a generation to the family, especially when no subfamily was involved.

As mentioned earlier, during the sample period subfamilies tended to replace secondary families. As reported in Table 3.7 the percentage of families with subfamilies increased throughout the sample period. If the percentage of secondary families out of the total number of families for each sample year is observed, an overall decreasing pattern emerges—in 1850, 14.6 percent of the families were secondary; in 1860, 14.2 percent; in 1870, 16.1 percent; and in 1880, 7.6 percent. With the exception of 1870 there is a reverse association between the trends of these two family types. The 1870 pattern is related to the effects of the Civil War—reduced fertility, broken homes, increased mobility, and the first enumeration of former slaves. The dramatically lower figure for secondary families in 1880 could result from the recount procedure—most of the subfamilies and other groups of family members with different surnames might have been counted as secondary families in the earlier censuses. As a check, all subfamilies for 1880 with a different surname from that of the family head were considered secondary families, but this only raised the figure from 7.6 percent to 8.9 percent. Because the subfamily definition is a bit more restrictive than the general family definition (see Appendix A), as a further check it was assumed that when at least two individual family members with a different surname from that of the head were in a household, they were a secondary family. (This, of course, would not always be the case even in the earlier censuses because individuals with a different surname from that of the family head frequently did not themselves share a common surname.) Even so, the percentage of secondary families for 1880 is only raised from 7.6 percent to 11.3 percent. This latter figure is still much lower than any of the others reported for the sample period and lends support to an overall pattern of a decline in the percentage of secondary families while the percentage of families with subfamilies is increasing. One factor attributing to the increase in family size for 1880 was the rather sharp decrease in the percentage of secondary families. (These tend to reduce family size averages.) Concomitant with this there was an increase in the percentage of subfamilies. (These usually increase family size averages.)

The last component to observe for the sample period is the percentage of households containing nonrelatives—individuals who are household members but are not a part of the primary family or any secondary family units in the household. The highest percentage of households containing nonrelatives was recorded for both 1850 and 1860 with 28.7 percent. For 1870 the figure declined to 26.5 percent, and for 1880 the figure declined drastically to 20.7 percent. Again, as a check, for 1880 it was assumed that all family relatives with different surnames from that of the family head were, in fact, nonrelatives. As a result, the figure jumps from 20.7 percent to 29.1 percent and is similar to the figures reported for the earlier censuses. This suggests that for these individuals, the greatest amount of error was likely to occur in the recount when determining their relationship to the household head. Many of these individuals were not a part of the head's or the head's spouse's immediate family (parents, children, siblings) and were (and would be for the earlier censuses) listed at the end of the family order. Individuals in this location presented difficulties when this study attempted to ascertain their family membership or lack of it (cf., Appendix C).

Two more sets of statistics help even further to define the problem. The percentage of household resident employees (those nonrelatives listing an occupation) during the sample period stayed fairly constant—16 percent for 1850, 17 percent for 1860, 19 percent for 1870, and 17 percent for 1880. However, the percentage of household lodgers (nonrelatives with no occupation listed) declined over the period with a sharp decline between 1870 and 1880. The figures for lodgers are 16 percent for 1850, 14 percent for 1860, 10 percent for 1870, and 5 percent for 1880. The decline in lodgers accounts for most of the decline in the percentage of households with nonrelatives. This is a result of the fact that the occupations listed for resident employees (farm laborer, domestic) were usually an additional indication of non-family status. Hence those individuals at the end of the household listing, having a different surname from that of the head, and with no occupation listed were usually determined to be lodgers. The indications are (based upon the 1880 data) that a number of these individuals so designated in the earlier censuses, were, in fact, family members. To keep this in perspective, it should be noted that this only affects a very small proportion of the total sample. These types of individuals are found only in about 5 percent of the sample. They do not add a marital pair or sub-family to a family unit because they are usually single individuals, and they do not usually add a generation. If they did, their location would be different in the family listing order. Those individuals with different surnames from that of the family head who might significantly change some of the structural statistics (a marital pair, subfamily, or add a generation) were the easiest ones to identify. Hence the greatest chance for error occurs for those individuals affecting the family statistics the least. Thus various kinds of support suggest that the recount procedure applied to the sample of households from 1850 to 1880 is accurate.

Typical Family Structure, 1850 to 1880

As the various family structural aspects have been presented, it has become clearer and clearer that, structurally, the family has changed very little throughout the sample period. Also the various structural aspects for the sample are similar to contemporary family structure which is contrary to the traditional perspective of family change. In fact, the typical family for each period would be almost identical.

Taken together, the sample data suggest a typical family for the later half of the nineteenth century. The commonly found family unit consisted only of a nuclear unit—the head's family of procreation. The family was headed by a married couple, one of which was designated the family head, and the only other family members present were children. There were usually two or less children in the family and no additional relatives were present—family members not a part of the head's family of procreation. This would apply to roughly 50 percent of the families for each of the sample years. To include a much larger percentage of the sample families, say around 80 percent, the unit would still be a nuclear one. The only change would be the presence of more children and not the presence of more relatives outside the head's family of procreation.

The presence of family relatives outside of the head's family of procreation occurred in only around 10 percent of the sample families. When these other relatives were present, they usually were the parents of the husband or wife of the nuclear family with a tendency toward the former. The addition of other types of relatives, such as siblings or a sibling's family, or more distant relatives was almost nonexistent.

For the contemporary period, the typical family would be almost identical, with the number of children being the largest change. The typical nuclear family observed at one point in time today would include only one child or, even more likely, no children.

The fact that the family structural aspects have changed very little during the sample period can be seen in Table 3.12. The mean differences vary less than five-tenths of a unit for the sample period and the percentage differences vary less than 5 percent. Because the change has not consistently gone in the same direction, these differences are even smaller when the 1850 figures are compared to the 1880 ones.

Each of the statistics chosen for Table 3.12, based upon the traditional expectations, were expected to decline over the sample period. If the statistics for a variable followed this expectation, the pattern of change was identified with an "A." The only variable to completely follow the expected pattern was the only

Table 3.12: Summary of Differences Between Household
and Family Structures, 1850 to 1880

Table Number	Subject	Percentage or Mean Range	Percentage Change or Mean Difference 1850-1880	Pattern of Change[a]	Year with Highest Figure
3.2	Household size	0.50	−0.50	A	1850
3.4	Family size	0.43	0.04	B	1880
3.6	Percentage of extended families	4.9%	4.9%	C	1880
3.7	Percentage of families with subfamilies	2.1%	2.1%	C	1880
3.8	Number of marital pairs per family	0.05	0.03	B	1880
3.9	Percentage of head-spouse families	4.1%	2.1%	B	1880
3.10	Percentage of male headed families	2.2%	−1.3%	B	1850
3.11	Number of children per family	0.42	−0.06	B	1850

Source: The tables listed in the first column on the left in this table.

a. Pattern definitions: A means a decline in the figure for each census. B means the figure first declines then increases. C means an increase in the figure for each census.

nonfamily variable included—household size. Most of the family variables followed pattern B. Hence all of the family variables except two first declined and then increased in incidence. These five family patterns declined for the first two censuses, and three of them declined again for the next census. But they all increased for the 1880 census. In fact, in three out of five cases the increase for 1880 was a rather dramatic one as the 1880 figure was larger than the one reported for 1850. The two remaining family variables followed pattern C by increasing in each census. This was a reversal of traditional expectations.

The data suggest that a number of interesting things occurred. First, there are the unexpected directions taken by the trends of the data. All the variables violate, to some extent, traditional expectations by either reversing their trend during the sample period or by displaying a completely opposite trend. Also of interest is the amount of change that took place between the censuses. The least amount of change occurred between the 1850 and the 1860 censuses. The only two exceptions were for percentage of families headed by a married couple and percentage of families headed by a male. For all family aspects except the percentage of extended families and percentages of families with subfamilies, the change represented a decrease. Between 1860 and 1870 the amount of change increased for all family aspects except for married couple-headed families and male-headed families. It is between these two censuses that the directions of the trends are the most divided. Only family size, number of children, and male-headed families display a decrease. As mentioned earlier, the disruptive effect of the Civil War period upon family structure (especially fertility) seems to be of primary importance here. The increases in the percentage of families that were extended and that included a subfamily also appear related to the war and possibly to the increased rate of urbanization and industrialization spurred on by it. The former disruptive effects might have brought about the family structure compensation factor mentioned earlier—in the absence of a spouse or children of the head, other relatives are more likely to be present. On the other hand, the latter processes might have brought about temporarily extended families which would aid families in their transition to an urban area. These services often included assistance in job placement, child care, and some economic support (or at least reduced expenses). But despite a larger change between these two decades, the changes were really not very dramatic and the effects of these factors were apparently not very widespread. The increase in the number of families headed by a married couple is unexpected, but it is only a small increase.

The changes between 1870 and 1880 are the biggest for all of the family aspects except one—male-headed families. In addition, all of the aspects show an increase in incidence from 1870. This is interesting because some previous changes are explained, to a certain degree, in terms of a complementary relationship between structural changes. Again the change in family size appears to be primarily due to an increase in the number of children. The increase in the number of children seems to result from a number of factors. First, in the late 1860s and early 1870s, there was a return to a higher fertility rate after the slump in the mid-1860s. Also, the disruptive effects of the Civil War were no longer in operation, i.e., the fact that children left home earlier than normal and that some never returned because of premature death or migration into another area. Other research has noted that in some areas in the United States during the 1880s there was a trend for more older children to remain in the household than was true in the 1850s (Bloomberg et al., 1971:23-25). Hence, an increase in the number of children per family size is expected. Whereas the differences between the changes for family size and number of children between 1850 to 1860 and 1860 to 1870 are fairly similar (the former is 0.01 and the latter is 0.04), the difference between 1870 and 1880 (0.07) is almost double the next largest difference. Thus, for 1880 the increase in the number of extended families and those families with subfamilies played its most important role, albeit a very small one, in helping increase family size during the sample period.

These increases in the number of extended families, families with subfamilies, and number of marital pairs per family need to be further explored. All of these show their most significant increases between 1870 and 1880. One factor already considered was the possible emergence of a help pattern with the temporary establishment of extended families. This pattern was followed for a number of different reasons. Bloomberg's et al. (1971) data suggest that in southern Michigan a much higher proportion of older children (over twenty-one) were residing in their parents' household in 1880 than 1850. In rural areas a disproportionate number of these older children were sons. Important considerations here were the reduction in the availability of frontier land and the waiting necessary for the inheritance of land. In the urban areas there was a disproportionate number of daughters, possibly waiting for marriage, among these older children. But even after marriage several reasons suggest a continued residence with one's parents. Sons expecting an inheritance could not afford to jeopardize their investment and future holdings by moving away from their parents' land. In urban areas there were also many economic advantages for a newly married couple living with one set of their parents at least temporarily (Anderson, 1971:140-144). In some cases economic reasons (for example, child care) were the basis for providing lodging for parents (usually just the widowed mother) of the head or the head's spouse. In fact, it was more common for single parents and other single relatives to live with a nuclear unit than for a household to be shared by two adult siblings and their families. This is suggested by the much larger increase in the percentage of extended families versus the percentage of families including subfamilies. Anderson (1971) found the provisions of lodging for widowed female parents (or sometimes other relatives) in exchange for child care fairly common in his English sample. This situation was particularly true in those urban-industrial areas where women (mothers) had an equal or better chance at employment than men.

Also showing an increase from the 1870 figures are the number of families headed by a married couple and the percentage of families headed by a male. Both increases appear related to the fact that the Civil War no longer had any ill effects plus the decrease in the proportion of secondary families in the 1880 sample. Secondary families usually have a higher proportion of single parent families and female-headed families.

Support for the findings from the 1850-1880 sample is provided by the research that has dealt with the families of various ethnic groups during the latter half of the nineteenth century. Furstenberg et al. (1973) compared the household and family structures for four ethnic groups—black, Irish, German, and native white Americans—located in the city of Philadelphia during the years 1850-1880. For each group the predominant family of residence form was nuclear and "only minor variations" existed between the four groups (p. 8). Overall, like this study's sample, the greatest incidence for extended families occurred in 1880 and not in 1850 (pp. 9-10). One aspect which did display a good deal of variation was the percentage of families headed by females. Black families were the most likely to be female headed (25 percent) and German families the least (8 percent). However, even these differences "diminish sharply under conditions of economic parity" (p. 12). The nineteenth century families of black Americans have recently received more attention than most other ethnic groups (cf., Cremin, 1974). In the numerous studies that have been completed the evidence again and again indicates the prevalence of the husband-wife nuclear family among both free and unfree black Americans throughout the nineteenth century (pp. 255-256). In fact, more variation regarding family structure has been demonstrated for occupational groups (families categorized by head's occupation) than by the comparisons of ethnic groups (Seward, 1976). Hence, the research in ethnic groups tends to support the representativeness of the sample.

It is clear that family structural characteristics have not changed dramatically during the sample period. Change has not always followed the expected trends, and some initial suggestions are made offering possible explanations. Some of these suggestions are based upon indications from the sample data, some from data collected by other researchers, and a few have been impressions gained from collecting the data. Obviously the situation is a complex one and is rendered even more complex by conflicting currents that affect the data.

An example of such a factor involves a simple measure of the family head's geographical mobility. Complete information was not available but it was possible to compare the family head's place of birth to his or her residence location at the time of the census enumeration. For place of birth the most specific information given was state, if within the United States, or region or state plus foreign country when outside the United States. Thus we could distinguish between those family heads that resided in the same state in which they were born, those who resided in a state contiguous to their state of birth, those who resided in a noncontiguous state within the United States, and those individuals born in a foreign country. Table 3.13 presents this information.

Table 3.13: Geographical Mobility of Family Head Based upon Place of Birth and Present Residence by Percentage: 1850 to 1880 Sample

Birth Place in Relation to Residence	1850	1860	1870	1880
Total Percentage	100.0	100.0	100.0	100.0
Same state	28.5 (26.4)[a]	28.4 (26.4)[a]	34.0 (33.6)[a]	37.5 (38.8)[a]
Contiguous state	15.0 (15.4)	15.1 (15.7)	11.7 (12.5)	11.0 (11.6)
Noncontiguous state	38.9 (46.1)	34.2 (37.4)	30.4 (33.1)	26.2 (28.3)
Foreign country	17.5 (12.2)	22.2 (20.4)	23.9 (20.8)	25.2 (21.3)

Source: Same as Table 3.2.
   a. Based upon a subsample of primary family households where the only residents of the households are primary family members.

Two interesting and somewhat contradictory trends appear to have occurred during the sample period. First, there was an increase in the proportion of family heads who resided at the time of enumeration in the same state in which they were born. Second, there was an increase in the proportion of family heads who were born in a foreign country. It can be argued that these trends had different effects upon family structure.

First the trends in mobility for the native-born Americans present a pattern different from that expected. The process of industrialization is supposed to increase and even necessitate geographical mobility as a result of the need for a mobile labor force. The trend here is in the opposite direction. In 1850 the typical (47 percent) pattern was for the native-born family head to reside in a state that was not adjacent to the state of his birth. By 1880 this was true for only a little more than a third of the native-born family heads (35 percent). On the other hand, by 1880 just slightly over half (50.1 percent) of the native-born family heads resided in the same state where they were born. This suggests that it was possibly easier and more likely that family members could maintain contact and actually have more of an opportunity for sharing households in 1880. This is supported in part by the sample data because the families of native-born heads residing in the same state as their birth were the most likely to include a subfamily (4 percent) and be extended (5 percent). In contrast the families of foreign-born heads were the least likely to include a subfamily (2 percent) and be extended (3 percent). Regrettably, information concerning in-state migration is not available and it would be foolish to try to deny the importance of migration from the rural areas to towns and cities. But in spite of this, the minimum evidence does seem to suggest a decline in migration for new lands on the frontier (the substantial decrease in the non-contiguous category). This was replaced by migration for other reasons (for example occupational) and usually involved shorter distances. Again, this means there might have been more opportunity, in addition to some of the reasons already cited, for an increase of families that were extended or contained a subfamily.

At the same time an increase occurred in the proportion of family heads born in a foreign country. The proportion increased from less than one-fifth (17.5 percent) of the sample families in 1850 to more than one-fourth (25.2 percent) in 1880. These families were the least likely to be extended or to include a sub-family but had the highest likelihood of being a secondary family. In fact, over 23 percent of the families with foreign-born heads were secondary units while only 10 percent of the families with native-born heads were secondary units. For the families with foreign-born heads the pressures that would affect family structural statistics were in contradiction to the pressures for the native-born Americans in the sample. At the same time these families might have increased the average number of children reported per family. While the native-born headed families had an average of 2.3 children, the foreign-born headed families had an average of 2.58 children. Bloomberg et al. (1971:41-43) also suggested such a pattern in their study. In the rural areas and towns of southern Michigan it was the native-born family population that showed the biggest decrease in the number of children when comparing statistics for 1850 to 1880. In the urban area (Detroit) the native-born population actually showed an increase in the number of children per family while the number of children for the foreign-born decreased. The latter decrease, however, was rather small and the averages were still larger than the averages reported for the native-born population residing outside of Detroit (in addition, the averages were almost identical to those native-born families residing in Detroit). Hence, the increase in immigrants during the sample period might have been a force that helped increase the average number of children per family. In particular, it played a most important role in the increase reported for 1880, although the possible role of native-born urban dwellers cannot be ignored.

Finally, a word concerning the only variable in Table 3.12 that followed the expected pattern—household size. The data tend to suggest a much stronger inverse relationship between household size and the processes of industrialization and urbanization than between these two processes and the various family aspects. Such factors as a higher standard of living, which allowed couples to purchase or live in their own home and reduced the necessity of taking in boarders for economic support, the separation of work or occupations from the home, including the disappearance of resident employees and apprentices in the family's household, and an increasing number of dwelling units available, help account for the inverse relationship (p. 33). These factors, resulting from the processes of industrialization and urbanization, were possibly more important to a reduction in household size than to a reduction in the incidence of the family aspects observed. With this in mind the next concern is to assess the effect of these two processes upon household size as well as upon the family changes presented in this chapter.

In summary, the various structural aspects of the family during the latter half of the nineteenth century have varied very little overall. But there have been changes, and, in a number of cases, unexpected ones. Thus, the next question is to determine the role of industrialization and urbanization in these changes. These processes, of course, have repeatedly been mentioned as bringing about dramatic changes in the family system.

Chapter 4

INDUSTRIALIZATION, URBANIZATION,

AND THE FAMILY

It is and has been a common contention that the processes of industrialization and urbanization have brought about important changes in the American Family as well as in the family systems of other nations. The impact ascribed to these two processes by many observers to explain family change and other societal changes has been little short of being an article of faith. This chapter is concerned with showing how close this contention is to social reality. As noted in Chapter 1, a great deal of literature supports this supposed relationship, but little of the literature has explored it in any depth. Even the most recent and most critical literature has done little to spell out the relationship, much less test it.

In the past there was a scarcity of reliable, historical, and quantitative data about the family in regard to the entire population. Most of the information preserved about the earlier family systems represents primarily the most wealthy and influential families. These families were frequently atypical. The data presented in this study are much more representative. Even the colonial data included representatives of every segment of the population although each study was usually limited to one community. The 1850 to 1880 sample covers the various geographical regions in the United States as they existed during the sample period, and includes family units at various economic and occupational levels. It was possible to select and reconstruct the structure of a group of individual family units who provide a representative cross-section of American society. The result was the documentation of historical baselines for family structure during the last half of the nineteenth century, as presented in the last chapter.

Additional information other than that needed to determine family structural aspects was available on the original census manuscript schedules. This information can be used to index the process of industrialization and urbanization. This chapter focuses upon the sample period from 1850 to 1880 because it offers the most direct way of measuring the effects of industrialization and urbanization upon family structure as measured by a number of variables.

In addition, because data are given from other time periods in this study and since it will be useful to put the sample period into perspective in terms of the developments in these two processes, another broader approach is also attempted. Hence, an attempt is made to put the development of these two processes into separate periods based upon some considerations previously mentioned in Chapter 1. Utilizing these separate periods, a broader historical comparison of household and family size is presented.

Family Structure during Three Stages
of Industrial and Urban Growth
in the United States

One way of assessing the effects of the industrialization and urbanization processes upon the family is to divide the history of the United States into the different periods of development for these two processes. When discussing the challenges of the supposed effects of these two processes upon the family in

Chapter 1, the arguments of Levy (1965) were presented in some detail. Although he presented his argument more in terms of a cross-cultural comparison, his types of societies can be applied to the historical development of a particular nation. For the United States, Levy's first type of society will be considered equivalent to the preindustrial period; his transitional society will be identified as the period during which the processes of industrialization and urbanization were rapidly developing; and his second type of society will consist of that period after which the maturity of these processes were reached, or the postindustrial period. The next concern is to set the time boundaries of these three different periods.

The development of industrialization and urbanization is obviously a continuous process rather than one that occurs in a distinct set of stages. But at least two factors suggest that one should ignore the obvious and attempt to set up stages. First, many writers have tried to make sense out of the development of the processes of industrialization and urbanization by attempting to identify periods of time which share some general characteristics, yet are different from other periods. Second, family studies frequently define the type of family or period being studied in terms of a stage or period related to industrialization or urbanization, e.g., the preindustrial family or the family during the preindustrial period are commonly used.

A number of indices can be used to suggest the boundaries of these periods. Several sources have suggested that the boundary between the preindustrial period and the industrial period lies somewhere in the beginning of the sample period. In the development of the United States, the 1850s are usually considered the beginning of the rapid acceleration and spread of the processes of industrialization and urbanization (Schneider, 1957:51-71); Wilensky and Lebeaux, 1958:49).

From the beginning, the American environment was free of many elements (e.g., feudal system, guilds, and entrenched social classes) which had hampered industrial growth elsewhere (Schneider, 1957:51-52). In addition, the physical and climatic conditions were also favorable to industrial growth (p. 51).

Another positive factor was the development of the "American spirit." Although some controversy exists over the reasons for this development (cf., Thernstrom, 1968), most observers agree that American industrial growth was "nourished from the beginning by a hard-driving, self-sacrificing, individualistic, optimistic, energetic, and even ruthless people" (Schneider, 1957:52). Rostow's (1960) stages of economic growth pointed out another element in favor of American industrial growth. He presented five stages of economic growth: traditional society, preconditions for take-off, take-off, drive to maturity, and age of high mass consumption. However, only the last four stages are relevant to the United States because it was "created mainly out of Britain [which was] already far along in the transitional process or the preconditions for take-off stage" (p. 17). Hence, many steps of economic development "through which other countries passed were skipped entirely" in America (Schneider, 1957:53).

Despite all these potentially favorable factors, American industrial growth did not immediately develop. In fact, some of these favorable factors initially "posed great barriers to industrial development." For example, the frontier, while contributing to the development of the American spirit, at the same time "acted as a huge drain, absorbing surplus population, [and] making the price of factory labor dear." Thus it took a long period of time before these favorable factors had their full effect. Although some temporary advancements in industrial growth occurred, the following factors assured very slow development: "high labor costs, poor transportation, uncertain and shifting markets, and a lack of native capital, an unstable currency, lack of credit institutions, an unskilled labor force and a backward technology" (p. 54). In addition to these factors, and in some ways more important, was the basic British policy toward its American colonies. The colonies were to be used as a marketplace for goods manufactured in Britain and as a source of raw materials for British industry. The American Revolution was partly a result of this economic policy. But the Revolution had varying effects upon industrial growth and the American victory did not result in a dramatic upsurge in American industry. It was not until the 1850s that the necessary factors seemed to jell and the most phenomenal growth in manufacturing was displayed (p. 55).

Hence the period from the inception of the American colonies up to the mid-nineteenth century is usually considered the pre-industrial period. Rostow (1960:38) also suggested this division when he considered the end of the preconditions for take-off stage and the beginning of the take-off stage for the United States as occurring between 1843 and 1860. This argument suggests that the colonial data and, perhaps, the sample data for 1850 in this study represent the preindustrial period. Other indices, as well, suggest these boundaries for the preindustrial period and indicate a period of relative stability for at least the first half of the nineteenth century. This is of some importance because only the 1850 data represent the nineteenth century for the preindustrial data.

Demographers (Davis, 1945:1-11) in their presentation of the demographic transition "theory" cite high birth and high mortality rates, which are relatively stable over a period of time, as characteristic of a preindustrial period. The mortality rate for the first half of the nineteenth century is seemingly stable according to Taeuber and Taeuber (1958) and no conclusive evidence exists of any decline in these rates. More recent work also appears to support this contention (Smith, 1973b). It is difficult to present comparable data on mortality rates during the colonial period, but a recent work (Vinovskis, 1972) suggested that, at least for Massachusetts, the mortality rates remained relatively constant throughout the colonial period until 1860. After this time, "declines in mortality seem to have been almost continuous" (Taeuber and Taeuber, 1958:269).

It is more difficult to support the existence of a stable pattern for fertility. As noted in Chapter 2, a decline in completed fertility took place during the second century of the colonial period. But many of these colonial figures, especially those from the seventeenth century, are higher than the estimates for completed fertility for the first half of the nineteenth century (Coale and Zelnik, 1963:36). Most of the lower colonial studies' figures reported for the eighteenth century are still higher than the national estimates presented for 1840 and 1850. Hence, the birth rate reached its highest levels during the period designated as preindustrial but there were some substantial fluctuations. Nevertheless, the lowest figure for the eighteenth century (Smith, 1972) was never topped again after the 1860s. Finally, the estimated completed fertility rate for the first half of the nineteenth century is at a rather stable level, with an overall gradual decline and a relatively large drop occurring between 1840 and 1850 (Coale and Zelnik, 1963:36). Thus, for birth and mortality rates some of the properties expected during a preindustrial period appear to have occurred.

Evidence presented in Table 4.1 provides some data on indices related to the growth of the processes of industrialization and urbanization. The first column reveals that during most of the

Table 4.1: Population Residing in Urban Areas and Labor Force Involved in Farming Occupations or Manufacturing plus Construction Occupations for the United States, by Percentage from 1820 to 1930

Year	Percentage of Urban Population	Percentage of Labor Force Farmers	Percentage of Labor Force Involved in Manufacturing and Construction	
1820	7.2	71.8	12.2	
1830	8.6	70.5	a	
1840	10.8	68.6	14.6	
1850	15.3	63.7	16.4	
1860	19.8	58.9	18.3	
1870	25.7	53.0	21.3[b]	23.2[c]
1880	28.2	49.4		23.0
1890	35.1	42.6		26.1
1900	39.7	37.5		27.5
1910	45.7	31.0		28.7
1920	51.2	27.0		31.4
1930	56.2	21.4		28.7

Source: United States: Bureau of the Census (1960a:9, 72, 74).
  a. Not available.
  b. Comparable to earlier years.
  c. Comparable to latter years.

first half of the nineteenth century, one-tenth or less of the United States' population resided in urban areas. The only exception is, of course, the 1850 figure, which also exhibits the largest increase from an earlier decade for this period. The second column indicates that the percentage of the labor force involved in farming was rather stable from 1820 to 1850 (with the change between 1840 and 1850 again being the most dramatic) and included at least two-thirds or more of the labor force. Less than one-sixth of the labor force was involved in manufacturing and construction types of occupations from 1820 to 1850 (column 3). Together these figures are indicative of a preindustrial period and most of them suggest a relatively stable period for the first half of the nineteenth century. However, some of the changes occurring in the statistics between 1840 and 1850 point out the difficulties involved in trying to establish definite boundaries for these periods and challenges the idea that the 1850s represent a "stable" period preceding industrialization. Rostow (1960:7-10) also supported these contentions when he dated his take-off stage as 1843-1860 instead cf using a single year. This period is used because different regions of the United States experienced expansion at different times (p. 38).

During the 1850s industrial growth seriously got started with both a disappearance of some previous limitations and a fuller realization of some of the advantages in the American environment. The 1850s witnessed a tremendous growth in manufacturing (e.g., the emergence of the factory) and a flood of immigrants who provided a cheap labor force. Newly discovered gold from California plus profits accumulated from a prosperous agriculture provided necessary capital. These factors launched the rapid development of American industry (Schneider, 1957: 55-64). In the 1860s a major political event—the Civil War— resulted in a new political coalition in control of government which enacted a program that "created the condition for a veritable explosion of American industry in the latter half of the nineteenth century" (p. 57). Other contributing conditions were the continuous stream of immigrants after the Civil War (cf., Table 3.13), a growing domestic market, the exploitation of

Western lands which provided large supplies and some surpluses of foods, and finally rapid technological developments. The result was the construction of a great industry between the years of 1860 and 1900 (p. 64). Rostow (1960:7-10) suggested an identical time period when dating his drive to maturity stage. More specifically, he noted that the period from 1868 to 1893 was the time during which the most rapid overall industrial growth occurred and large scale industry matured in the United States (p. 40). Consequently, the 1860 to 1900 period is considered equivalent to the industrial or transition period and to Levy's third type of society (also called transitional). Because it is argued that the postindustrial period did not start until 1920, the 1910 data will also be considered part of the industrialization period.

Various statistical indices can help describe this period. The stable period for the mortality rate during the first half of the nineteenth century was followed by an almost continuous decline from the 1850s until the present (Taeuber and Taeuber, 1958: 269). The decline, however, occurred at different rates. Available data (United States: Bureau of the Census, 1960a:30) suggests that the decline for the rest of the nineteenth century was fairly gradual. In contrast, the first two decades of the twentieth century showed a decline almost double this earlier one (p. 27). As suggested earlier the estimated completed fertility rate (Coale and Zelnik, 1963:36) made two rather large drops between 1830 and 1840 and 1840 and 1850. In fact, the drop between 1840 and 1850 was the largest one (although not the largest change) between any two decades for which data are available. This decline continued throughout the designated industrial period and did show an overall larger decrease than that occurring between 1800 and 1850. The decline in total fertility for the entire period (1860-1910) was a little less than two children per mother. Overall it was a fairly consistent decline with the sharpest decline occurring in the mid-1860s.

The mortality and fertility rates, then, went in the expected direction, but their particular paces of change were not the ones suggested by the demographic transition pattern. The pace of the declines seemed to be turned around. The birth rate exhibited the most rapid decline prior to and during the beginning of the period and not toward the end. On the other hand, the mortality rate had a long gradual decline with the most rapid rate occurring at the beginning of the twentieth century, not at the beginning of the industrialization period. Hence the population surplus expected to result from the demographic transition pattern had to come from another source, namely immigration.

The data in Table 4.1 suggests, however, that the industrialization period was one of rapid transition, especially during the first three decades. In 1850 only 15 percent of the population lived in urban areas, but by 1860 it had jumped to almost 20 percent. This rate continued to increase at a rapid pace; hence at the end of the period—in 1910—nearly a majority of the population (46 percent) was involved. The percentage of the labor force who were farmers was declining rapidly. In 1860 almost three-fifths of the labor force were engaged in farming. By 1910, however, this proportion had been almost cut in half, with only 31 percent of the labor force still classified as farmers. The percentage of the labor force involved in manufacturing and construction also increased during this period although not as dramatically as the others. Comparisons are complicated somewhat by the fact that the basis for classification changed in 1870 (see table); however, there does appear to be a steadier increase in the proportion of these occupations and a more dramatic change than occurred for the earlier period. The latter change may seem less dramatic than the others but, of course, industrialization means changes in other occupational areas as well. The later figures (1920 and 1930) in Table 4.1 indicate that the percentage of the labor force involved in manufacturing and construction had almost reached its peak by 1910. In fact, the 1940 figure shows a slight decline from the 1930 one. Also, the proportion of persons involved in manufacturing out of the total labor force employed in nonagricultural establishments has steadily decreased from 39 percent in 1920 to 31 percent in 1960 (United States: Bureau of the Census, 1960a:74; 1965:14). While this decline in the proportion of manufacturing occupations was going on, increases occurred in the proportion of the labor force employed in wholesale and retail trade, services, and government. Hence, the major expansion in the labor force for manufacturing took place during the industrialization period.

Finally, the remaining period (1920 to 1970) is considered equivalent to the postindustrial period and Levy's second type of society. By the beginning of this period the foundation for modern industry in America had been established. A huge transportation network (railroads) had been constructed, "great heavy industries had been built, [and] the major urban-industrial centers had been created and were being rapidly filled by a labor force entirely dependent on industry for livelihood" (Schneider, 1957:63-64). Rostow (1960:10) termed this period, his fifth and final stage, the age of high mass-consumption, where "the leading sectors [of the economy] shifts toward durable consumers' goods and services."

As expected, the number of persons engaged in farming continued to decline throughout this period. On the other hand, those individuals involved in manufacturing and transportation industries showed an increase in actual numbers but a steady decline in their proportion of the total labor force (United States: Bureau of the Census, 1960a:73). Enlarging their proportion of the labor force were, in increasing order of importance, the construction industry, wholesale and retail trade, services, and the government. This can also be seen by noting the changes occurring at different job levels for the period 1920 to 1960. Skilled workers increased in numbers during the period about in proportion to increases in the total number of persons included in the labor force. On the other hand, semiskilled workers (operatives and kindred workers) more than doubled the increase in the total labor force, and professional people and office workers increased three times more rapidly than the labor force did as a whole (p. 74). Hence the "era of the professional technicial, and the skilled and semiskilled worker had arrived" (Rostow, 1960:76-77).

The mortality rate for the postindustrial period, like the prior period, is one of overall decline. In 1920 the number of deaths per 1,000 people of the population was 13.0. By 1960 this figure had dropped to 9.6 (United States: Bureau of the Census, 1960a:27; 1965:6). The trend was fairly consistent and dropped rather slowly throughout the period. The total decline for the period was less then the ones occurring between 1900 (17.2) and 1920 (13.0). The birth rate also shows an overall pattern of slow decline. Based upon the figures reported by Coale and Zelnik (1963:22-23) for the white population, the rate reported for 1920 was 25.0. By 1960 the rate had only dropped to 22.2. For the total population during this period the figures were a bit higher; the overall difference was larger but the trend was still the same (United States: Bureau of the Census, 1960a:23; 1965:4). Despite this overall pattern the birth rate was not as stable as the mortality rate. In particular, the birth rate started to drop more rapidly during the 1920s, especially during the latter half. It continued this drop during the first half of the 1930s and remained at this low level (around 17.0) until the early 1940s when it began to rise. During the latter half of the 1940s the rate increased to levels that equalled those reached in the 1910s and early 1920s. Hence, the birth rate displays a curvilinear pattern during this period. While the pattern exhibited by the mortality rate is one expected according to the demographic transition model, the birth rate does not follow the expected pattern.

Thus, the history of the United States can be divided into three different periods in reference to its industrialization process with accompanying urbanization. As the periods were presented, a number of instances arose which did not fit the expected pattern. Overall, there is some support for the existence of these periods although the setting of specific year boundaries does not seem to make sense, especially between the preindustrial and the industrial period.

One way to assess the influence of the industrial and urbanization processes upon the family would be to establish how much its structural aspects have changed throughout these three development periods. Chapters 2, 3, and 5 in this study attempt to provide the descriptive data that make this possible. But a problem arises because the data are still very spotty. They add information on the structure of the family historically, but

Table 4.2: Household, Family, and Primary Family Mean Sizes for American Colonies and United States: Sample and National Data

Year	Household	Family	Primary Family
1689[a]	5.99	5.32	
1774[a]	6.14	5.61	
1790[b]	5.79		
1850	5.55[b]	4.79[c]	5.28[c]
1860	5.28[b]	4.69[c]	5.05[c]
1870	5.09[b]	4.40[c]	4.78[c]
1880	5.04[b]	4.83[c]	5.04[c]
1890	4.93[b]		
1900	4.76[b]		
1910	4.54[b]		
1920	4.34[b]		
1930	4.11[b]		4.11[d]
1940	3.77[b]		3.88[d]
1950	3.39[e]	3.54[d]	3.69[d]
1960	3.33[f]	3.65[g]	
1970	3.07[h]	(3.57)[h]	3.57[h]

a. Source: Demos (1968:41-54).

b. Source: United States: Bureau of the Census (1960a:16).

c. Source: Tables 3.4 and 3.5. The primary family data in this instance refers to the subsample of primary family household used in Chapter 3.

d. Source: United States: Bureau of the Census (1955:2A-11, 31).

e. Source: United States: Bureau of the Census (1953a:1-8).

f. Source: United States: Bureau of the Census (1963a:21).

g. Source: United States: Bureau of the Census (1963b:465).

h. Because of the small number, no secondary families were counted. Source: United States Bureau of the Census (1973a:7, 23).

there are still a lot of important and large gaps. To reduce this problem to a minimum and still make an historical comparison, the aspects of family size and household size will be the only ones observed. (For the other family aspects there are even less data available.) Table 4.2 presents a collection of comparable data on these aspects. Most of these mean sizes are presented elsewhere in this work. The sources include previously reported national data, samples presented in other works, and this study's 1850 to 1880 sample. Because of definitional changes and differences, family data are given for all families (column 2) including both primary and secondary units (the head of a primary also heads the household in which the family resides) and for primary units only (column 3). For 1930 and 1940 only data on primary families are available, and in 1970 secondary families (because of their small number) were not counted as family units.

Despite the incompleteness of the data, a few observations are in order. There is obviously an overall pattern of decline for both household and family size; however, some differences should be noted. Household size appears to be more consistent in its decline and is reduced by almost 50 percent over the entire period. Family size is a bit more irregular in its decline and is reduced by only about 35 percent over the entire period. In other words, average household size is reduced by roughly three persons while the family was reduced by only two persons. This decline in family size (as well as household size) is less than some had suggested (see Chapter 1) and again demonstrates the smaller overall variability and gradual nature of the change. This gradual change also questions the usefulness of presenting different industrialization (and urbanization) periods and suggests the relative lack of effect these processes had upon family and household size. The indications are that no sharp distinctions occurred between the three periods. Again as the data in Chapter 3 suggested, household size appears to be more responsive to the processes of industrialization and urbanization than is family size, because household size continues to drop consistently while family size shows a more fluctuating pattern by increasing when it should be dropping and declining overall much less.

Family size breaks the pattern of consistent decline both in the sample period (1850 to 1880) and in 1960. Apparently, a key explanation of this is the change in the number of children in the family, which is primarily a reflection of the fertility rate. As indicated in Chapter 3 most of the change in family size results from a decline in the number of children in the family. Hence, roughly, as the fertility rate fluctuated so did family size.

The historical relationship between household and family size is also relevant. Whereas household size starts out consistently larger than family size for the early data, household size is smaller than family size for the last four decades. Resident employees and lodgers, some of whom composed secondary families, were frequently a part of earlier households. Their disappearance meant a decline in household size. This in turn meant an increasing similarity between household size (which more and more only included a primary family) and family size. The decline of household size below family size from 1950 to 1970 was made possibly by an increase in the number of households containing only one individual. The percentage of one-person households has gone from almost being nonexistent in the colonial period to including nearly one-fifth of the households in 1970.

The trend towards more similarity between overall family size (which includes both primary and secondary families in its calculation) and primary family size relates to this change in residence patterns as well. In particular, this resulted from the almost total disappearance from the household of secondary families composed of resident employees or lodgers. Secondary families are usually much smaller on the average than primary families. Consequently, the total size figure for the sample period (1850 to 1880) was reduced by as much as one half a person because secondary families were included in the calculation of the total family size figure. During the sample period roughly 15 percent of the total number of families were secondary. In 1970 less than one-fifth of one percent of the total number of families would have been secondary. As a result, secondary families were not even counted. But even before 1970 the reduction in secondary families is reflected in the increasing similarity between total family size and primary family size.

The data in Table 4.2 suggest that historical change has been rather gradual for household size and family size, especially the latter. Considering that these aspects are the ones which have changed more than other family aspects (see Chapter 3), suggest the limited use of historical comparisons for these other aspects even if the data were available. Which is another way of implying the lack of impact of industrialization and urbanization upon the family.

Finally, despite the references to and uses of industrialization and urbanization periods in the family literature, it is apparent that the usefulness of these periods in explaining family change is extremely limited for several reasons. First there was difficulty setting specific dates for the time boundaries of these periods. Second the change for household and family size was so gradual that these development periods really offered no help in explaining the changes that did take place. This would be even more the case for the other family aspects. As this gradual change in the family and the changes in the urban population and labor force (Table 4.1) suggest, it really makes more sense to deal with industrialization and urbanization as a continuous process. The statistical analysis at the end of this chapter carries out such an approach.

In defense of this discussion, a minimal outline of industrial development in the United States will be useful later when some specific measures of industrialization and urbanization are defined. In addition, this discussion indicates that the sample of 1850 to 1880 covers a period of dramatic change for several indices for the processses of industrialization and urbanization. At this point, it appears fruitless to pursue any further historical comparisons; hence, the best course seems to be the utilization of the more detailed sample data (described in Chapter 3) from the nineteenth century. Because this is a national sample, it is possible to deal with the problem of regional differences in industrial and urban growth which might have resulted in a different rate of change for family structural aspects in each region.

Family Structural Aspects by Region

It has been implied thus far that the years estimated to be the boundaries of the industrialization period were fairly appropriate for all areas within the United States. A number of indices, however, suggest this was not the case. In Chapter 3, when justifying the sampling procedure, it was intimated that differences existed between the Northeast, North Central, and Southern regions in regard to population, population growth, and type of economy. In the 1850 census, the South stratum led slightly in population with the Northeast stratum second. The North

Central stratum was the least populated. Over the years sampled, the population of the North Central region increased at the highest rate with the Northeast second. The South exhibited the lowest rate of growth. Throughout the sample period, the economy of the Northeast stratum relied most heavily upon mining and the manufacture of goods. The Northeast region had already experienced marked expansion and development of manufacturing and railways in the 1840's prior to the sample period (Rostow, 1960:38). These initial developments of industrialization did not occur in the North Central (Midwest) region until one decade later. Hence it was the North Central stratum which had in 1850 relied heavily upon agricultural and lumber products that experienced the greatest change in economy. As time progressed, its economy became more like the Northeast stratum. The South's economy changed very little as it relied predominantly upon its agricultural products throughout the sample period. The South lagged very far behind the other regions in its economic development. Because of the type of economy developed in the South, which was first an appendage to the cotton mills in England then New England, plus the effects of the Civil War, the marked expansion of industrial development for the South was delayed until the 1930s (p. 67). This was almost a century later than for the Northeast region.

These distinctions between the strata suggest a type of homogeneity within each stratum. Based upon the existence of differential rates of industrialization for the strata, a comparison between them should provide additional information relevant to the concern with the industrialization process. In particular, it is possible that part of the reason for the "gradual" change noted in Table 4.2 might be "regional blurring." Hence, the possible "dramatic" effects of industrialization and urbanization were tempered by a different progress of these processes in the various regions. This can be tested by observing the family structural aspects covered in Chapter 3 and breaking them down by the different regions for the sample period.

The expectation would be that the effects of industrialization and urbanization should first be evident in the Northeast followed by the North Central Region, and realized last in the South. The South developed so far behind the other two regions that little effect should be noticed during the sample period. In other words, the South should be the most stable in its family structural aspects during the sample period.

HOUSEHOLD AND FAMILY SIZE

Household size data for the various regions are presented in Table 4.3. Surprisingly, the more rural South and North Central regions have the lowest mean household size, with the Northeast having the largest. This is the case for each decade, and the difference between the Northeast region and the other two regions is roughly four-fifths of a person for all decades except 1880, where this difference is nearly cut in half. Throughout the sample period there is a great similarity between the figures for the North Central and Southern regions. The biggest difference (which is only two-tenths) occurred in 1870. The lower figure for the South possibly resulted from two related factors: the heavier toll in the Civil War, and the first enumeration of former slaves. This is demonstrated by the fact that the number of secondary families in the South for 1870 was more than double the incidence found in the two earlier decades and the decade (1880) that followed. Also, despite this dramatic increase in secondary families, household size still decreased in the South in 1870.

Table 4.3: Household Mean Size for Regions, 1850-1880

Region	1850	1860	1870	1880
Northeast	6.36	6.25	5.93	5.58
North Central	5.63	5.37	5.25	5.17
South	5.50	5.43	5.01	5.22
Total	5.83	5.68	5.40	5.33

Source: United States: Bureau of the Census, Seventh Census Population Schedules, Eighth Census Population Schedules, Ninth Census Population Schedules, and Tenth Census Population Schedules, Microfilm Publication Numbers M704, M653, M593, and T9. Washington, D.C.: National Archives and Records Service. (For rolls used, see references.)

Secondary families also played a role in the higher sizes reported for the Northeast region. The Northeast region had nearly three times as many secondary families throughout the sample period as did other regions. The role of immigration cannot be ignored, especially as Boston, Massachusetts, and Brooklyn, New York were part of the sample in this region. Secondary families were the least important in the North Central region because by 1880 less than 2 percent of the total number of families were secondary ones. The pattern for the North Central region in this respect seems more in line with one expected effect of industrialization—the decline of secondary as well as subfamilies in the household. (Later evidence will show a lack of decline in subfamilies.)

In general, the pattern for each region was fairly similar to the national or total pattern—an overall steady decline. Two noteworthy exceptions are the sharper decline in the Northeast for the last three decades and the sharp decline in the South between 1860 and 1870, followed by the only increase in household size throughout the period. The overall decline for the Northeast is larger than for the other two regions, in fact, almost double, which might be due to some aspects of the industrialization and urbanization processes. (Some of the measures introduced later had their highest association with household size in the Northeast.) The sharpest decline occurred in the South and appears to be related to the factors mentioned above—the devastation of the Civil War and the first enumeration of former slaves.

On the other hand family size for the different regions presents a contrasting picture to household size. These data are presented

Table 4.4: Family Mean Size for Regions, 1850-1880

Region	1850	1860	1870	1880
Northeast	4.45	4.41	4.20-	4.52
North Central	5.01	4.82	4.59	5.00
South	5.00	4.90	4.46	5.03

Source: United States: Bureau of the Census, Seventh Census Population Schedules, Eighth Census Population Schedules, Ninth Census Population Schedules, and Tenth Census Population Schedules, Microfilm Publication Numbers M704, M653, M593, and T9. Washington, D.C.: National Archives and Records Service. (For rolls used, see references.)

in Table 4.4. In this case the Northeast region is the smallest of the three but again, with the exception of 1870, the North Central and the Southern regions are almost identical. Another contrast is the lack of overall decline, and like the national or total figure, there is a decline in each region for the first three decades followed by an increase in 1880. For each region the 1880 figure is almost identical to the 1850 one. In contrast to expectations, the Northeast, which should show effects of industrialization and urbanization more, actually displays the largest increase when the 1880 figures are compared to the 1850 figures. The South's and North Central's patterns might suggest conformity to expectations but the Northeast's figure should have continued to decrease. As with household size, the South shows the largest decline between 1860 and 1870. Of course, all of the regions decline in 1870 to their lowest point due to the lower fertility rate in the 1860s and, to some extent, the other effects of the Civil War, but obviously the South was most affected. However, the South recovered (or increased its size) faster than the other regions.

The role of secondary families must be mentioned since these played a role in the smaller sizes for the Northeast region. Again, the role of immigration was important as well as the living arrangement patterns followed in the large urban areas— tenement housing.

Finally, it should be added that the decline in household size can, only to a limited extend, be related to the changes in family size. The overall change in family size is much less and the variation between regions is smaller.

Hence data for the three different regions do not add any support to the supposed effects of industrialization and urbanization. Family size is lower overall in the Northeast region, which is expected, but, at the same time, the pattern is the most stable of the three regions, which is unexpected. Not only is the Northeast the most stable but the 1880 size actually shows an increase over the 1850 figure. The smaller sizes are partly due to the larger proportion of secondary families in the Northeast region. Thus, for family size the expected size difference was present but the trend the figure followed was unexpected.

With household size an opposite conclusion seems appropriate—the differences in size among the regions were in unexpected directions but the trends for the regions were similar to what was expected. Again, the idea is supported that of the two size aspects, household size is more responsive to the two processes under study. The conclusions here are much the same as those in Chapter 3. However, the effects of the Civil War upon the family, particularly for the South, does receive additional support.

GENERATIONAL COMPOSITION

For generational composition both the percentage of extended families and the percentage of families with subfamilies by region is considered. Data on the former aspect are presented in Table 4.5. The trend for each region is much the same as the total tend—an overall increase in the percentage of extended families with the figure in 1880 almost triple the 1850 figure. While the Northeast region had the smallest family size, it was certainly not due to having fewer extended families. It is the Northeast region which has the highest percentage of extended families throughout the sample period and not the more rural and less industrialized North Central and Southern regions. The higher percentage in the Northeast is curious in light of the fact that the highest percentage of secondary families were also present in this region. In addition, the trend of the percentages for each region is the opposite from what is expected—it increases each decade. As mentioned in Chapter 3, some undercounting was probably involved prior to 1880 for this aspect, but the first three decades which are comparable still show this increasing trend.

Table 4.5: Percentage of Extended Families by Region, 1850-1880

Region	1850	1860	1870	1880
Northeast	3.4	3.8	4.2	8.8
North Central	1.8	1.7	3.1	6.3
South	1.8	2.6	2.9	6.5
Total	2.4	2.7	3.4	7.3

Source: Same as Table 4.3.

Table 4.6: Percentage of Families with Subfamilies by Region, 1850-1880

Region	1850	1860	1870	1880
Northeast	2.7	3.0	3.7	4.7
North Central	0.8	1.4	2.1	3.1
South	1.6	2.2	3.1	4.0
Total	1.9	2.3	3.0	4.0

Source: Same as Table 4.3.

For the percentage of families with subfamilies (Table 4.6) the possibility of undercounting was reduced to a minimum. But just as with extended families, the regional trends are almost identical. Again, the Northeast has the largest percentages; the pattern is one of an increasing percentage for each decade. One new development is that the North Central region clearly emerges as the region with the lowest percentage. For the previously presented aspects the figures for the South and North Central regions have been very similar.

For generational composition two important exceptions to the anticipated effects of industrialization and urbanization emerge. First, the region that is the most urban and industrialized (Northeast) has the highest percentage of "extended" families, and the percentage actually increases with each decade. This seems to add even more support to Anderson's (1971) contention that there was an increase in the incidence of extended families during the industrialization period. In addition, the availability of cheap land and other opportunities that acted as inducements to move on played a part in the much lower incidences for the North Central region. The second exception is that the other two regions, as well as the Northeast, showed an increase in the percentages for each decade. Also, the rate of increase for each region is roughly the same. Even the South fails to display a disrupted pattern for the 1870s.

HEAD-SPOUSE FAMILIES

Table 4.7 presents data on the percentage of families which were headed by married couples, i.e., both husband and wife were present in the household. In fact, each region's trend is unique, and only the trend for the North Central region follows the total (national) trend of first declining and then slowly increasing for the last two decades. The Northeast's pattern is identical except that the figure declines in 1880 instead of increasing. The South deviates, again probably due largely to the effects of the Civil War, in that while the other two regions increased in the 1870s, it decreased.

Also the North Central region has the highest percentage of families headed by a married couple. This is in line with the expectation (Burch, 1967:363) that other family members outside the nuclear family tend to be present when the head's and/or children were absent. This ties in with the data presented in Tables 4.5 and 4.6 which show that the North Central region had the lowest percentage of "extended" families—extended in generations—or families with subfamilies. Further, the lower percentages for the Northeast shown in Table 4.7 are also in line with this argument. The decline in 1880 for the Northeast might also be taken as support for the expected effects of industrialization and urbanization—a lower level and decrease in the percentage of families headed by a married couple. This argument is, however, strongly challenged by the South's data. The South's percentages of "extended" families are similar to the low levels for the North Central region, but the percentage of couple-headed families in the South is substantially lower than in either of the other two regions. If this lower level were limited primarily to the 1870s, it would be more understandable, but

Table 4.7: Percentage of Head-Spouse Families by Region, 1850-1880

Region	1850	1860	1870	1880
Northeast	84.5	82.3	85.8	82.8
North Central	87.1	84.8	86.9	90.9
South	78.1	76.8	72.6	83.3
Total	83.4	81.4	82.5	85.5

Source: Same as Table 4.3.

the same lower level is displayed for both 1850 and 1860. Hence, the varying trends offer conflicting support for the traditional expectations.

NUMBER OF CHILDREN

The remaining concern is with the number of children per family for the various regions. These data are presented in Table 4.8. Much of the discussion on regional family sizes also applies to the regional patterns for the number of children per family. As expected, the Northeast has the lowest figure but, again, it is the most stable region throughout the sample period. It shows an increase in 1880 which results in a figure almost identical to the 1850 figure. The North Central and Southern regions are again almost identical throughout the sample period. As with family size, it is the South which shows the greatest change. It is closely followed by the North Central region. Taken together the trends for each region seem more similar to the total trend than was the case for family size. Also, if the dip taken by all regions in 1870 is removed, the means for each region has remained almost identical. The dip in 1870, although the largest for the South, seems to suggest that a drop in fertility occurred in all the regions. Finally, as suggested in Chapter 3, most of the changes in family size appear to be accounted for by the changes in the number of children per family.

In summary, presenting the data by separate regions does not uncover varying trends for each region. The process of "regional blurring" did not exist, and virtually no support was found for the traditional argument concerning the effects of

Table 4.8: Number of Children per Family by Region, 1850-1880

Region	1850	1860	1870	1880
Northeast	2.40	2.36	2.13	2.38
North Central	2.97	2.87	2.53	2.88
South	2.99	2.85	2.41	2.89
Total	2.76	2.67	2.34	2.70

Source: Same as Table 4.3.

industrialization and urbanization upon the family. There were different regional levels of incidences on the different family aspects observed, but these differences did not usually follow traditional expectations. In fact, household size, generational composition, and the incidence of couple-headed families did not follow these expectations; only family size and number of children did. More important was the fact that the trends for each region were almost identical to the national or total trends with the exception of couple-headed families. In addition these trends frequently went in opposite directions from those traditionally expected. In a number of cases the most urban and industrialized region (Northeast) displayed the characteristics (at least had the highest incidences) thought to be associated with more rural and nonindustrial areas. The argument given the most support is the role of the Civil War in affecting family aspects, as suggested by the South's trends.

The Family's Relationship
to the Industrialization and
the Urbanization Processes

As mentioned in the beginning of this chapter, data available from the census' manuscript schedules and reports for the 1850 to 1880 sample period can be used as more direct indices of industrialization and urbanization. Describing the relationship between these two processes and the family will provide a basis for the indices that are used.

Of the two processes industrialization seems to be the easiest to relate to the family and probably offers the most direct relationship. The industrialization process will be dealt with first.

The family as an institutionalized unit fulfills certain functions in society through the performance of some of its activities. The performance of these activities by the familial institution affects other social institutions which, together with the family, make up the social system. The relationship goes both ways because the activities performed by other social institutions, in turn, have certain effects upon the family. These relationships can be conceived of as a series of interchanges (cf., Bell and Vogel, 1960:7-20; Parsons and Bales, 1955:33-34). A fit or stability is achieved between social institutions by the achievement of a balance in these interchanges; a balance is achieved when the contributions made by one social institution are reciprocated by contributions from other social institutions. This balance, which is not necessarily perfect, will be affected as the activities of a social institution change. As a result, the balance is usually in a state of flux and not stable. The interchanges are not necessarily in the form of concrete goods but may also be behavioral actions or responses.

The particular set of interchanges of interest here are those occurring between the family and the economy. Today the economic institution is that part of the social system which is involved with the production and distribution of goods and services. At one time the production and distribution of goods and services was a part of the activities performed by the family, but no longer. Most contemporary families are now primarily concerned with the consumption of these goods and services. Of course this transition of the family from a self-sufficient unit to a unit of consumption is considered one of the most important changes resulting from industrialization. This transition is believed to have brought about additional changes in many other family patterns.

The contemporary family must acquire the necessary goods and services for its survival from the economy. In exchange for these goods and services, the family contributes to the economy resources which usually take the form of money. To obtain the necessary monetary resources in another interchange, the family provides labor for the economy. The laborer then performs a certain work role or occupation in exchange for wages. This latter interchange—labor for the economy and wages for the family—is considered one of the most influential links between the familial institution and the economy.

As was pointed out in the discussion concerning industrial growth in the United States, the characteristics and the activities of the economy change as a result of the industrialization process.

As noted in Chapter 1, many have argued (cf., Parsons and Bales, 1955:3-35; Parsons, 1964:151-198; Goode, 1963:366-380) that because of the changes in the characteristics and activities of the economy, the familial institution must change accordingly. Again, the general contention is that the small nuclear type of family is necessitated by certain characteristics of industrialization.

One characteristic of an industrial society that is assumed to be related to family structural changes is occupationally induced geographical mobility. In other words, for many individuals in an industrialized society to pursue, maintain, or improve their occupational position, they must be able to move geographically. Any kin group wider than the nuclear family would inhibit geographical mobility; therefore, the nuclear family becomes the unit of mobility. In addition, geographical mobility makes it difficult to keep in contact with kin which, in turn, further reduces the importance and frequency of kin relationships. The reproduction function is also affected since larger families (more children) inhibit geographical mobility. A related argument is that in industrial society children are an economic liability rather than an asset.

Another characteristic of industrialization related to occupations is the creation of many new and different kinds of jobs—division of labor. As a result there is less intergenerational occupational stability, and kin are generally more occupationally differentiated. This, in turn, reduces the probability of any individual being able to help a kinsman in his job because, in most cases, they will be in a different occupation. Hence, this aids in the breakdown of kinship networks.

As Harris (1969:93-121) pointed out, there are two factors which are implicitly assumed in discussions of the relationship between industrialization and the family but are usually never explicitly mentioned. The two factors are "degree of job differentiation and an increase in the level of skill" (p. 111). With the increase in job diversity that exists and with the higher degree of skill required, fewer workers can fill each other's job. What is happening, suggests Harris, is a reduction in the "substitutability" of many jobs as a nation industrializes. The lower the level of "substitutability" between jobs or the more fixed the occupations, the more difficult it becomes to "fit" men into jobs. In addition, the more difficult it is to fill jobs, the more necessary it will be to allot jobs purely on the basis of merit and the more moving around of workers and their families will be involved.

Hence, as the industrialization process expands in a society, more differentiated jobs will emerge that demand increasingly more specialized skill for their successful performance. In addition to this trend, it should also be noted that in some segments of the economy, management often attempts to reduce job differentiation and the level of specialized skill. There is a fear that the more jobs are differentiated and the skill level increased, the more difficult it will become to control the laborers holding these jobs. One alternative has been to increasingly automate various jobs which, in many cases, reduce the skill and differentiation of the affected occupations if they are not completely eliminated altogether. But, on the other hand, greater skills are often required by the "survivors." Thus, not all occupational levels in society are going to be affected in the same manner. Some occupations show an increase in differentiation and skill, e.g., technicians, while others show a decrease in differentiation and skill, e.g., certain types of operatives. The decrease in differentiation for the latter refers to the ability to perform many other jobs at the same level without any increase in skill or training being necessary. Althouth a job may require a highly specific operation, such as a position on an assembly line, transfer to other positions similar in occupational level should be no more demanding.

The "effects" of industrialization should be more important for the more differentiated jobs that emerge and demand more specialized skill for their successful performance. It is argued that as more individuals "fit" into these more differentiated occupations, demands are made upon the individual laborer which, in turn, affect his family. It therefore follows that no matter what phase of industrialization a society is in, there should be great variation between different occupational levels in terms of the degree of skill required and the extent of job differentiation. In addition, there should be differences in family patterns between occupational categories which might lead to a number of different family types (or different family aspects), all associated with industrialization. The occupation of the head of the family unit, then, becomes an important variable. The effects of industrialization should be the greatest when the "substitutability" of the head of the family is the lowest—the more fixed the occupation. Using various measures based upon occupational levels and the occupational structure in the United States during the sample period should provide some measure of the effect, if any, of industrialization upon the family unit.

The urbanization process is more difficult to relate directly to the family. At the same time it is difficult to separate the urbanization process from industrialization. It was the process of urbanization that brought together the concentrated labor force necessary for industrial growth. A combination of factors helped provide the necessary labor force; the increased mechanization of agriculture which meant a reduction in employment needs, the disappearance of cheap land on the frontier, and the promise for greater economic security in urban areas "through higher wages and more attractive working conditions" (Lantz and Snyder, 1969:46-48). These factors worked together to shift a once dispersed rural population to one that became increasingly concentrated and congested.

The urban environment is thought to contain a number of elements that have had an impact upon the family. First of all, the family was no longer able to be as productive and self-sufficient as it was in its prior rural settings. As described above, the family became primarily a unit of consumption. As a result, many of the needs of family members were satisfied by agencies outside the home. In addition, many remaining household duties were substantially simplified as a result of mechanization derived from an advancing technology. This meant that less time and energy was needed to provide for the family's survival, and more time was available to family members for devotion to other activities. Consequently, more emphasis was placed upon individual needs and interests. This often resulted in challenges to traditional family authority and relationships.

Because the urban setting provided various opportunities for individuals to pursue and satisfy their needs outside the family, family members were involved in various groups and situations that involved interaction with many nonfamily members. Whether it was working, education, or other types of experiences, these nonfamily members were frequently individuals with different beliefs and backgrounds. Many individuals were constantly confronted by new and different beliefs and behavior in their relationships outside the family. Hence, the heterogeneity of the urban population tended to challenge one's belief in the exclusiveness of their particular family patterns. Their family patterns were obviously just one of many possibilities. Added to this was the fact that religious and community control was no longer as strong as in the past. In part this was due to the increasing amount of anonymity that was possible as the urban areas became larger and even more dense. Thus, it is argued, urban areas provided an environment which contained several elements conducive to the weakening of family patterns that had been a part of the rural setting. For structural aspects, this meant that the extended family was no longer necessary or desired; the number of children per family was also lowered. The necessity of both these aspects was assumed to disappear in the urban setting.

As families settled in urban areas they were exposed to a different environment composed of new and often challenging elements. A number of indices relating to the process of urbanization are available for the sample period, and allow at least some measure of the possible effects of this process upon family structure.

INDUSTRIALIZATION AND URBANIZATION INDICES

The final way to attempt a measurement of the effects of industrialization and urbanization upon the family is to use indices related to these processes which can also be related to the families from the 1850 to 1880 sample as described in Chapter 3.

Beside the information used on the original manuscript census schedules for the family structural aspects, information is available that can be used as indices of these two processes. With these data plus some from published reports for the sample period it is possible to locate each of the sample families in an environment based upon the values of the various industrialization and urbanization indices or variables. The purpose of this exploration is to see if, as any of the industrialization and urbanization variables varied, there was any associated variation in family structure. In other words, did families in highly industrialized-urbanized areas exhibit different structural characteristics than families in more rural and less industrialized areas? A wide range of scores were possible on each industrialization and urbanization variable, hence the family's environment was not classified simply as either industrialized-urbanized or nonindustrialized-rural but could take on a value located somewhere on the possible range of scores. The more family structural variables increased in the same direction as the industrialization-urbanization variables, the higher the association between them. If one accepts the view that industrialization and urbanization had a significant impact upon family structure, one can expect the occurrence of tangible associations.

Although limited by the information available from either census manuscript schedules or published census reports, a number of indices for both industrialization and urbanization are available. When different sources are used, the directness of the indices vary. Some of the indices related directly to a family unit, e.g., the occupation of family head, while others were less direct and reflected characteristics that a family unit shared with a group of other families, e.g., population density of county in which the sample family resided.

A good deal of information was available in regard to industrialization that dealt with occupational aspects. This seems particularly fortunate in view of the emphasis placed upon the changes in the occupational structure that resulted from industrialization. The occupations performed by family members provided a rather direct link between the economy (industrialization) and the family. The most direct measure used was the occupation of the family head. This information was the basis for two different variables. The first was *occupational group,* which placed the family head's occupation in one of nine categories based upon the Edward's classification code system developed for the U.S. Bureau of the Census (Edwards, 1943; Miller, 1970: 172-193), although some nineteenth century occupations were not only difficult to define but also difficult to categorize. The second use of the family head's occupation was an attempt to measure its *occupational substitutability* as suggested by Harris (1969). Two different criteria were used to determine the substitutability of the various occupational groups—the nine occupational groups used for the previous variable. One criterion was the amount of specialization needed for a particular occupation, that is, specialization in terms of training or preparation needed before fulfilling a particular occupation. The other criterion was the amount of differentiation involved in an occupation's work role responsibilities, that is, the specificity or departmentalization of an occupation's duties. For both criteria a simple dichotomy was made between a high and low level. It was then proposed that the following occupational groups represent a rank order of increasing substitutability (those at the top are the most highly specialized and differentiated):

	Differentiation	Specialization
Professionals and technical workers	high	high
Clerical and sales workers	high	low
Operatives	high	low
Business managers, officials, and proprietors	low	high
Craftsmen and foremen	low	high
Service workers including domestic workers	low	low
Unskilled laborers including farmers	low	low

Three additional variables related to occupations were used. Two of these were based upon the occupational structure for the state in which a sample family resided. The first variable was the percentage of *nonextractive occupations* in each sample state. The value was determined by the percentage of individuals not involved in agricultural, mining, fishing, forestry, or logging occupations out of the total number listed in the state where a sample family was located. The second variable was the percentage of individuals involved in *mining occupations* out of the total number of occupations listed for a given sample state. It was assumed that the higher the percentages for each of these variables, the higher the level of industrialization in a state.

The final variable related to occupations provides a measure of the occupational structure at the county or parish level. This variable is the percentage of the *county's labor force involved in manufacturing*. Regrettably, a complete list of occupations by county was not available as was the case for states, but from manufacturing census reports the number of manufacturing establishments and their number of employees by county was available (for all sample censuses except 1850). Because the total labor force was not known for each county, to get a value for this variable, the number of persons employed in manufacturing establishments was divided into the county's potential labor force—25 percent of its population. This 25 percent figure was based upon a rough estimate of the percentage of the total U.S. population that listed an occupation in each of the census years for the sample period.

The final industrialization variable was the *family head's geographical mobility*. This was determined by comparing the family head's place of birth to place of residence at the time the census was taken (see Table 3.13). These are the six variables which are available and are considered to be indices of the industrialization process.

For the urbanization process a number of indices available help to locate the sample families in particular urban environments. The first and most direct measure was the family's *household location*. A sample household was classified into one of the following categories: urban, nonurban community, rural nonfarm, and rural farm.

The remaining urbanization variables dealt with the population characteristics of the counties in which the sample families resided. The first variable was the *population density of the county*. The second variable was the *population growth of the county*, which was determined by finding the percentage of increase or decrease in the county's population since the previous census year. For the last three variables, the percentage of the county's population as it was distributed among three different categories was determined. The three categories (variables) included the following: percentage of *urban population in county*, percentage of *nonurban community population in county*, and percentage *of rural population in county*. These six variables were used to measure different aspects of urbanization in terms of population distribution.

Besides these twelve variables, two additional ones were available and used. The first was *time*. As both industrialization and urbanization were developing at an accelerated pace during the sample period, time itself became a variable worth consideration. The other variable was *real estate value*. The value for this variable was based upon the amount reported on the original census manuscript schedules for real estate property owned by the family head (this information was available for all but the 1880 census).

For each sample household and family from either the 1850, 1860, 1870, and 1880 census manuscript schedules, a value for each variable was determined. The sources of the data for the variables varied. A number of the variables (occupational group, occupational substitutability, family head's geographical mobility, household location, and real estate value) were available on the original census manuscript schedules which were used in collecting the family data. For the remaining variables (except time since its value was based upon the decade the census was taken), the necessary information was gathered from a number of census reports which were published for each census during the sample period. Most of the information is available from the population summary reports published by the U.S. Bureau of the Census (1853; 1864; 1872a; 1883a). For information concerning a sample county's manufacturers and employees, the summary reports utilized were based upon a census of such establishments taken along with the population censuses (United States: Bureau of the Census, 1866; 1872b; 1883b).

FINDINGS

An analysis was carried out to ascertain the relationship between the industrialization-urbanization variables and the family structural aspects for the sample period. In this relationship each of the latter variables—family structural aspects—were considered the dependent variables while the former variables were the independent variables. The analysis used both Pearson product-moment correlations and multiple regression analysis. In both cases the computer programs used to carry out the statistical computation were a part of the *Statistical Package for the Social Sciences* (SPSS) unit (Nie, Bent, and Hull, 1970:143-156, 174-195).

The zero-order correlation coefficients between the independent and dependent variables are presented in Table 4.9. An immediate impression is the lack of high correlation coefficients. The highest coefficient is only .17, which is between the variables of household size and the population density of the sample counties. The vast majority of correlations fall below the .10 level; in fact, only 16 out of the 112 correlations presented are either equal to or higher than the .10 level. On the other hand, the majority of the correlation coefficients (69 out of 112) are significant by at least the .01 level. With the large sample size (9,600 households and 10,999 families) involved here, the size of the correlation needed to be statistically significant is drastically reduced (as demonstrated in Table 4.9, a correlation coefficient of .03 can be statistically significant). Hence, more important than the number of significant correlations are the consistently low correlation coefficients plus the lack of uniformity in the direction of the associations. An initial conclusion is that the presumed effects of the processes of industrialization and urbanization upon the family as measured by these variables seem to be mixed and very weak. It must be remembered that the selection of

Table 4.9: Zero-Order Correlations Between Household-Family Structural Aspects and Indices of Industrialization and Urbanization (Listwise Deletion, Pearson's Product-Moment)

Industrialization Variables	Household-Family Aspects							
	Household Size	Family Size	Extended Families	Marital Pairs	Number of Subfamilies	Number of Children	Head-Spouse Families	Sex of Family Head
Occupational group	.01	-.10*	-.05*	.00	-.01	-.10*	.00	-.02
Occupational substitutability	.02	-.09*	-.05*	-.07*	.00	-.10*	.08*	.09*
Percentage of non-extractive occupations in state	-.02	-.11*	.01	.01	.04*	-.12*	-.01	-.04*
Percentage of mining occupations in state	-.04*	.00	-.01	.04*	-.02	.00	.05*	-.02
Family head's geographical mobility	.06*	.04*	-.01	.00	-.04*	.06*	.01	.00
Percentage of county labor in manufacturing	-.01	-.11*	.01	.00	.06*	-.13*	-.03*	-.04*

Table 4.9 (Continued)

Urbanization Variables	Household Size	Family Size	Extended Families	Marital Pairs	Number of Subfamilies	Number of Children	Head-Spouse Families	Sex of Family Head
Household location	.02	−.13*	−.02	−.07*	.02	−.13*	−.07*	−.13*
County population density	.17*	−.02	.04*	−.05*	.01	−.03*	−.06*	−.07*
County population growth	.01	−.02	.00	.01	−.03*	.03*	.02	.04*
Urban population of county	.13*	−.05*	.02	−.06*	.01	−.06*	−.06*	−.06*
Community population of county	−.02	.05*	.01	.02	−.05*	.06*	.04*	.01
Rural population of county	.13*	−.03*	.02	−.05*	−.01	−.04*	−.04*	−.06*
Remaining Variables								
Time	−.08*	−.06*	.04*	.07*	.04*	−.08*	−.08*	−.14*
Real estate value	.11*	.05*	−.02	.05*	−.02	.05*	.06*	.10*

*Correlation is significant by at least the .01 level. Due to the large sample size many were significant by at least the .001 level.

these particular variables was based primarily upon their availability and not their ability to represent either industrialization or urbanization. There is little doubt, however, that these variables are a part of or at least a result of these processes.

In Table 4.9, a positive correlation means that as an industrialization or urbanization variable changes in the direction expected during the development of industrialization or urbanization, household-family aspects tend to increase in size or incidence. For negative correlations, the household-family aspects decline in size or incidence as the independent variables meaure an increase in the development of industrialization and urbanization. All variables were either coded or their signs were later adjusted so that the direction of change, whether increasing (e.g., urban population) or decreasing (e.g., rural population) in value, was the expected change resulting from or a part of the industrialization and urbanization processes.

The expectation, based upon the believed effects of industrialization and urbanization, would be all negative correlations with the higher correlation coefficients indicating which variables had the strongest association. But not only are the correlations rather low, many have a positive correlation. None of the indices used here emerges as having an important effect upon the structure of the family.

Despite the lack of larger and entirely negative correlation coefficients, a number of general observations should be made. Although no completely consistent patterns occurred, three family aspects had a more uniform pattern (mostly negative correlations) and higher correlations than others. These were *family size, number of children,* and *sex of family head.* (For the last variable it is assumed that a reduction in the percentage of male-headed families should result from industrialization and urbanization.) Of these three variables, *number of children* had the highest correlations (only .13). This was closely followed by *family size.* As suggested in the earlier chapter, the strong association between these two aspects was supported. Although very minimal, the industrialization and urbanization processes apparently had their biggest effect upon the number of children residing in the family. The majority of correlations were negative for the *sex of the family head* variable, but the largest and most significant correlations resulted from the urbanization variables. Hence, the more urban an area, the lower the percentage of male-headed families and the greater the percent of female-headed families. An important consideration here was the drop in the male-headed households between 1860 and 1870, particularly in the South (notice the high –.14 correlation for time). Since the sample used for these coefficients was selective (because of listwise deletion), this drop became much more important.

The coefficients for the remaining family aspects simply add more credence to the association between number of children and family size and, by contrast, make the latter's correlations appear more important. A clear majority of the correlations for these other aspects is under the .05 level and, in each case, most of the coefficients are positive and not negative as expected. Finally, a word about *household size*—only five of the fourteen coefficients are negative. Those variables having the strongest negative coefficients with family aspects are positively associated with household size. As with *sex of family head*, the strongest correlations for *household size* are with the urbanization variables. But in this case the coefficients are positive and not negative.

In computing Pearson's product-moment correlation coefficients, two options are available concerning the inclusion or exclusion of each sample case. The options allow for different methods of handling missing values for the various variables. In this study's sample, the percentage of missing values varies greatly from variable to variable. For example, *family size* is available for every family unit while the information for *occupational group*—family head's occupation—had sometimes never been recorded on the original manuscript schedules. The two options for dealing with missing values are listwise deletion and pairwise deletion of cases. Listwise deletion and the option applied to calculate the correlation coefficients for Table 4.9 cause a sample case to be omitted from the calculations of all coefficients if one or more of its twenty-two variable values are missing. Hence the variable with the largest number of missing values establishes the maximum number of cases used in the computation. For the coefficients in Table 4.9, only a little over 50 percent (53.1) of the cases (5,873) were used in these computations. Pairwise deletion involves the deletion of a sample case from the computation for a given coefficient when either one of the variables involved has a missing value, but the sample case is still included in the computations for all other coefficients where complete information is present. In this instance, the number of cases used for a specific coefficient fluctuates from all the sample cases (10,999) to only 6,578 of the cases. For the sake of comparison, the correlation coefficients based upon pairwise deletion are presented in Table 4.10.

Obviously, a number of differences exist between the correlation coefficients presented in Table 4.10 and those presented in Table 4.9. First of all, a number of much higher correlation coefficients are found in Table 4.10. Several of the coefficients show an increase over their counterpart in Table 4.9. Second, more of the coefficients in Table 4.10 are significant than in Table 4.9, but this was expected because the coefficients in Table 4.10 are based upon a larger number of cases. Although increases in the strength for some of the coefficients made them statistically significant.

The differences between the coefficients for the two tables should not be overly emphasized and a closer examination is warranted. While some of the coefficients in Table 4.10 increased substantially over their counterpart in Table 4.9, the majority either remained the same or changed very little. Most of the change that occurred was either equal to or less than a .03 (regardless of sign) difference. While in most cases this change resulted from a higher correlation coefficient in Table 4.10, for many there was actually a lower coefficient level or number in Table 4.10 regardless of sign. The coefficients for the family aspects of *family size, extended families,* and *number of subfamilies* remained fairly similar for both computations. Even for the four remaining family aspects, *marital pairs, number of children, head-spouse families,* and *sex of family head,* most of the equivalent coefficients in both tables were quite similar to one

Table 4.10: Zero-Order Correlations Between Household-Family Structural Aspects and Indices of Industrialization and Urbanization (Pairwise Deletion, Pearson's Product-Moment)

Industrialization Indices	Household Size	Family Size	Extended Families	Marital Pairs	Number of Subfamilies	Number of Children	Head-Spouse Families	Sex of Family Head
			Household-Family Aspects					
Occupational group	–.10*	–.12*	–.06*	–.20*	–.03*	–.22*	.30*	.35*
Occupational substitutability	–.12*	–.11*	–.07*	–.20*	–.03*	–.24*	.41*	.51*
Percentage of non-extractive occupations in state	.06*	–.11*	.01	.02*	.03*	–.10*	.01	.00
Percentage of mining occupations in state	–.03*	.02	.04*	.04*	.00	.02*	.03*	.02
Family head's geographical mobility	.16*	.04*	.01	.15*	–.02	.14*	–.17*	–.20*
Percentage of county labor in manufacturing	.05*	–.10*	–.01	.02*	.03*	–.10*	–.01	–.02

Table 4.10 (Continued)

Urbanization Indices	Household Size	Family Size	Extended Families	Marital Pairs	Number of Subfamilies	Number of Children	Head-Spouse Families	Sex of Family Head
Household location	.11*	-.17*	-.06*	-.06*	.00	-.15*	-.05*	-.05*
County's population density	.24*	-.08*	-.01	-.02	.00	-.06*	-.05*	-.05*
County's population growth	.02	.02	.00	.02	-.03*	.03*	.01	.02
Urban population of county	.21*	-.10*	-.03*	-.02*	.00	-.09*	-.03*	-.03*
Community population of county	-.04*	.07*	.04*	.03*	-.03*	.07*	.03*	.02
Rural population of county	.22*	-.10*	-.03	-.02	.02	-.08*	-.03*	-.03*
Other Indices								
Time	-.07*	-.01	.07*	.03*	.05*	-.02*	.02	-.01
Real estate value	.12*	.05*	-.02	.03*	-.01	.06*	.04*	.06*

*Correlation is significant by at least the .01 level.

151

another. The coefficients which exhibited the most dramatic changes all result from the same three independent variables— *occupational group, occupational substitutability,* and *family head's geographical mobility.* Hence, for all of the urbanization variables and for half of the industrialization variables, the equivalent coefficients were quite similar in both tables even for those family aspects that exhibited the greatest change. Because *occupational group* and *occupational substitutability* were based upon the same raw data—family head's occupation—and were only coded differently, they essentially duplicated one another, which added even more support to the similarity between the correlation coefficients in both tables.

It also is possible to identify the characteristics held in common by a group of families who would have been excluded in the listwise deletion computation (Table 4.9) but included in the pairwise deletion computation. The group consisted of female-headed households with the spouse absent but with children present. The occupations listed for these women in most cases were keeping house, keeping boarders, or farming, all of which are at the bottom of the occupational scale utilized. In the pairwise deletion computation for the occupational coefficients these family units (sample cases) would tend to be included primarily in the last two decades of the sample (1870 and 1880). This results from the various methods used in carrying out the census' instructions when the occupations for family members were initially recorded and the fact that the instructions issued by the census varied. In 1850 and 1860 occupations were only to be recorded for male family members over the age of fifteen, although in some areas occupations were listed for the female heads of families. For 1870 the occupations for family members of both sexes over the age of ten were to be listed, although frequently no occupations were listed for females. In 1880, with almost no exception, all adult members of the family had an occupation listed. Hence, female-headed families were likely to be excluded in the earlier censuses and likely to be included for the last two censuses, especially for 1880. The inclusion of female-headed families who had an occupation listed for the head in the pairwise deletion computation helps account for a large part of the more dramatic differences that occurred between the equivalent coefficients from the two tables. As the mobility variable confirms, these female family heads also tended to be less geographically mobile. These same family units had the greatest likelihood of having missing data from one or more variables.

Household size is the aspect showing the biggest difference between the two tables. In almost every case, the equivalent coefficient increases, as shown in Table 4.10, although half of the coefficients for the independent variables remain similar to the coefficients in Table 4.9. For the industrialization variables the biggest differences occur for the same three variables that exhibited the largest change for the family aspects. To some extent the same argument applied here. In addition, a number of urbanization variables also display a big change—*household location, population density, urban population,* and *rural population* (the last two urbanization variables essentially duplicate one another as a result of their complementary relationship). Again a group of households can be identified which were excluded from the listwise deletion computations (Table 4.9) and account for much of the differences in coefficients. These are the single person households, which were excluded because no family data was reported for the sample cases. As the change in coefficients suggests, these single person households were more common in rural areas, tended to have an occupation on the lower end of the scale (usually farming), and were less geographically mobile than other household heads.

The time variable is the only one that shows a consistent decrease from Table 4.9 to Table 4.10. This is due primarily to the fact that a real estate value was not recorded on the manuscript census schedules for 1880, which resulted in the exclusion of all 1880 cases when using listwise deletion. The largest drops occurred for the *head-spouse families* and *sex of family head* variables. These resulted from the relatively sharp decline in these aspects in 1870 and a higher rate of inclusion for the 1880 sample of female-headed families. Finally, the inclusion of the 1880 sample cases in the pairwise deletion computations (Table 4.10) reduced the coefficients for all other aspects because frequently the incidences for these household-family aspects in 1880 returned to a level more similar to those for 1850 and 1860. This suggests that most of the low correlations reported in Table 4.9 were actually exaggerated due to the use of the listwise deletion option. Hence, many of the "larger" correlations in Table 4.9 were, in fact, exaggerating the "association" between the family aspects and the industrialization-urbanization variables.

The next step was to perform a type of multivariate analysis upon the data that takes into account the interrelationships among the independent variables. The decision was made to use listwise deletion in the computation of the statistics for this analysis, despite the large reduction in sample cases used in the computation. When comparing the coefficients in Table 4.9 and 4.10, it is assumed that the correlation coefficients based upon a listwise deletion adequately represent the relationships between the variables being studied. In addition, using listwise deletion ensures that all coefficients are based upon the same set of cases.

Only those independent variables that appeared to have the strongest association with the household-family aspects (dependent variables) were used in this analysis. The logical independence of the variables, the coefficients in Table 4.9, and the Beta values from a multiple regression run that included all the independent variables were used to decide upon a reduced number of variables. The resulting list of nine independent variables with their Beta values for each dependent variable and the R^2 value resulting from all of the independent variables are presented in Table 4.11.

The R-square values at the bottom of Table 4.11 can be interpreted as that proportion of the variance in a household-family aspect, which is accounted for by the nine industrialization-urbanization variables included in the regression equation. The R-square values vary from relatively low to almost nonexistent levels. *Household size* has the largest value, but for this aspect only 6 percent of its variance is explained by the nine independent variables. The fact that this figure is almost double the next largest R-square value was unexpected based upon the zero-order coefficients presented in Table 4.9. Although household size had

Table 4.11: Relationship Between Industrialization-Urbanization Variables and Household-Family Based upon Multiple-Regression Analysis

Independent Variables	Household Size	Family Size	Extended Families	Number of Marital Pairs	Number of Subfamilies	Number of Children	Head-Spouse Families	Sex of Family Head
Occupational group	−.0062	−.0354*	−.0492*	.0445*	−.0237	−.0447*	.0533*	.0634*
Percentage of nonextractive occupation in state	−.0488*	−.0572*	−.010	.0559*	−.0012	−.0496*	.0498*	.0271
Percentage of labor force in manufacturing	−.0611*	−.0694*	.0064	.0051	.0561*	−.0855*	−.0196	.0101
Household location	−.062*	−.1064*	−.0173	−.085*	.0175	−.0907*	−.0922*	−.1745*
Population density of county	.2801*	.1091*	.0679*	−.0518*	−.0375*	.1101*	−.0355*	−.0931*
Population growth of county	−.0278	−.0101	.0065	.0008	−.0201	−.0056	.0038	.0081
Urban population in county	−.0194	−.234	−.0196	.0203	.0165	−.0365	.015	.1180*
Time	−.0089	−.0042	.0365*	−.070*	.0228	−.0137	−.0755*	−.1248*
Real estate value	.1204*	.0318	.0009	−.006	.0071	.0346	−.005	.0038
$R^2 =$	.0617	.0313	.006	.0121	.0049	.0345	.0143	.0356

*These Beta values either would round off to or exceed a .04 level.

the largest single coefficient in Table 4.9, some of the family aspects, especially family size, had consistently higher coefficients for the various independent variables. Hence the multiple-regression analysis of these same identical sample cases tends to support the contention that household size is affected more (but not very much) by the industrialization-urbanization processes than are any of the various family aspects.

The Beta values can be interpreted as indicative of the relative importance of each independent variable in relation to the dependent variable. To interpret the sign of the Beta values with confidence, these values should be roughly twice as large as the standard error value. Most of the Beta coefficients in Table 4.11 do not meet this criterion. Those Betas which were most likely to exceed their standard error value are designated by an asterisk. The use of such a low level is justified in part by the large sample size. For household size five Beta values exceeded the .04 level.

For the family aspects there are two different groups in regard to their R-square values. For the first group—*family size* (.03), *number of children* (.03), and *sex of family head* (.036)—the amount of variance explained by the independent variables is about one half (around 3 percent of what was explained for household size). For the first two family aspects not only are the R-square values nearly alike but the Beta values are also very similar. In addition, for each variable the same five independent variables have Beta values surpassing the .04 level. For the *sex of the family head* the R-square value is the highest of these three family aspects. Because listwise deletion resulted in the elimination of a certain type of sample case—female headed families in the earlier censuses—the R-square value for the *sex of the family head* variable is exaggerated. The high Beta value reported for the *time* variable supports this contention. As with the other two family aspects there are five Beta values which either equal or exceed the .04 level.

For the second group of family aspects—*extended families, number of marital pairs, number of subfamilies,* and *head-spouse families*—only 1 percent or less of the variance in these four aspects was explained by the nine independent variables. In addition, fewer Beta values for each aspect went beyond the .04 level and not one of the Beta values reached the .10 level.

The R-square values in Table 4.11 tend to give little or no support to the contended effects of industrialization and urbanization upon the family. Overall, the values indicate that almost no variance is explained by the variables selected. Although three of the family aspects display at least some association with these processes, the association is almost nonexistent for the majority (the remaining four). Again *family size* and *number of children* emerge as the variables having the highest association of all the family aspects being studied.

Finally, a word about the independent variables. Four of the nine variables emerge with the highest Beta values. Although the effect of the industrialization process upon family change has been emphasized in various arguments outlined in Chapter 1 and supported by the coefficients in Table 4.9, in this analysis, two of the urbanization variables emerge as the best predictors (highest Beta values) of changes for the household-family aspects. *Household location* and *population density of county* are the two independent variables which have the highest Beta values and their Betas consistently surpass the .04 level.

It must be emphasized though that both the R-square values and the Beta values are still much lower than conventional contentions would lead us to expect. The results of the multiple regression analysis challenge the supposed dramatic effects of industrialization and urbanization upon family structure. Some relationship exist but it is very minimal, and for some family aspects the relationship appears to be almost nonexistent.

Summary

This chapter assesses in a number of different ways the relationship between a number of household-family aspects and the processes of urbanization and industrialization. There is little doubt that some aspects have changed over time, although in a number of cases these have changed much less than or in the opposite direction of what has traditionally been expected. This chapter's analysis shows that for the change which did occur, industrialization and urbanization played only a very minor role. One reason for the lack of a strong relationship was that some of the family aspects have varied very little over time. Related to this stability is the fact that the relationship of industrialization and urbanization to the family's structure have varied among the many structural aspects considered. As suggested in Chapter 3 and further supported here, the three household-family aspects showing at least some relationship to the two processes are *household size, number of children per family,* and *family size,* which are listed in the descending order of importance. But even for these variables the relationship is much weaker than expected.

Chapter 5

CONTEMPORARY AMERICAN FAMILY STRUCTURE

The Postindustrial Family

This chapter presents data on the structure of the contemporary American family. It is based upon the 1950, 1960, and 1970 decennial enumerations taken by the U.S. Bureau of the Census. The family aspects and descriptive data presented are comparable to those in Chapters 2 and 3. To insure this, data for the contemporary period are limited to the last three censuses because earlier census data would not be comparable. As noted in Chapter 3, the definition of family applied by the U.S. Bureau of the Census has varied throughout its history. Only the data collected after 1947, when the last definitional change was made, are based upon a definition identical to the one utilized in gathering the previously presented data on the family of residence —any group of two or more persons who share the same household and are related by blood, marriage or adoption.

The data consist of the national census statistics for the entire population of the United States. As the census has developed historically, the population has grown tremendously; consquently the same detailed set of information has not always been elicited from each and every household surveyed by the census. Almost all the household-family data presented in the tables for this chapter are based upon a sample from the total households enumerated and the sample statistics have been adjusted to represent the total population. These samples varied in size from 20 to one percent of the total number of households. When possible, the same census sample was used for all of the family aspects presented. Since this was not always feasible, the N values and other statistics vary somewhat throughout the tables though the differences that result for the household-family statistics from different samples are minimal. For example, two different samples were utilized for the 1960 data because all the information needed was not available from one sample. However, for some of the characteristics, summary statistics were reported for each sample and they were in very close agreement (United States: Bureau of the Census, 1963a: XIII) as evidenced by only a .02 mean difference in family size between the two samples—one reported a mean of 3.63 (1963a) and other, a mean of 3.65 (1963b). (For a discussion of sampling variability and the procedures used by the Census Bureau to collect these samples, see the sources from which the data are drawn. These will either provide the required information or supply a reference.)

Family Structure

Data for the contemporary period on household and family aspects, based on the 1950, 1960, and 1970 U.S. Bureau of the Census' population enumerations, are shown in the tables provided below.

HOUSEHOLD SIZE

The number of households, their percentage distribution by size, and the measures of central tendency for the United States population for the last three censuses are presented in Table 5.1. Like the pattern for the nineteenth century figures, household size declined gradually over the three contemporary decades. The

Table 5.1: Number of Households, and Percentage Distribution by Size, 1950-1970

Size of Household	1950	1960	1970
All Households	42,826,000	53,019,457	63,573,042
Percentage	100.0	100.0	100.0
1 person	9.3	13.3	19.6
2 persons	28.1	28.1	28.5
3 persons	22.8	18.9	16.7
4 persons	18.4	17.2	15.2
5 persons	10.4	11.1	9.7
6 persons	5.3	5.9	5.3
7 persons	2.7 (5.8)	2.7 (5.6)	5.0
8 persons	1.4	1.4	
9 persons or more	1.7	1.5	
Modal size	2.00	2.00	2.00
Median size	3.05	2.95	2.62
Mean size	3.39	3.33	3.07

Source: United States: Bureau of the Census (1953a:1-8; 1963a:21; 1973a:7).

overall decline for the means was about three-tenths of a person, with the most change occurring between the 1960 and the 1970 censuses. The size categories that brought about the decline were much different from those for the nineteenth century. The decline for the 1850 to 1880 sample was due primarily to a reduction in the number of the largest households, i.e., the ten-person and eleven-person-or-more categories, which are almost nonexistent in the contemporary period. Furthermore, the percentage of households for all categories beyond three persons remained relatively stable throughout the three contemporary decades. The decline in the size for the 1950 to 1970 data was primarily due to a rapid increase in single person households which more than doubles during this period. This rather high and growing percentage of single person households resulted in a household average size figure that was lower than the average family size figure for the first time in American history. The increase in single person households was probably related to a number of factors which included the following: more available dwelling units with more residences specifically designed for single person inhabitation; a longer life expectancy for the population; and a rising expectation and opportunity for individuals to maintain a separate residence when they are no longer actively involved in a nuclear family. The last factor refers to the increasing tendency for off-spring to leave their family of orientation by the time of their marriage or, in many cases, to leave home prior to marriage in order to establish economic independence. A factor contributing to this change has been the growing emancipation of children. An increasing amount of stress upon individualism and independence has supported this emancipation. Manifestations of this change include expectations that young people gain their education (i.e., secondary socialization), economic independence (i.e., holding down a job), and residential independence outside the parental home. This latter manifestation creates additional smaller households while it diminishes the size of parental households. Also, the increasing emphasis upon the values of individualism and independence probably resulted in a decreasing tendency for grandparents to move into the homes of their children. These individuals both young and old, then, provided an increase in the proportion of smaller and, in many cases, single person households. In addition, a larger proportion of parents surviving beyond the time when their children leave home increased the proportion of smaller households. Finally, another important factor was the sharp decrease in the number of lodgers and servants (unrelated to the primary family) in the household. As these individuals disappeared from the dwellings of other families, they frequently established their own households, which also contributed to the increasing proportion of small households. Thus a wide variety of living arrangement patterns contributed to the decline in household size.

FAMILY SIZE

The number of families, their percentage distribution by size, and measures of central tendency from the 1950, 1960, and 1970 censuses are presented in Table 5.2. The 1970 data offer a slight change in the basis for the family statistics because only primary family units were counted. The decision to make this change was

Table 5.2: Number of Families, and Percentage Distribution
by Size, 1950-1970

Size of Family	1950	1960	1970
All Families	38,453,391	45,128,397	51,142,862
Percentage	100.0	100.0	100.0
2 persons	33.5	32.7	35.4
3 persons	24.8	21.6	20.8
4 persons	20.0	19.1	18.9
5 persons	10.8	12.8	12.0
6 persons	5.3	6.7	6.6
7 persons or more	5.6	6.3	6.2
Modal size	2.00	2.00	2.00
Median size	3.16	3.30	3.20
Mean size	3.54	3.65	3.57

Source: United States: Bureau of the Census (1955:2A-31; 1963b:1-465; 1973a:23).

based upon the small number of secondary families (95,000) that existed in 1969 according to the Current Population Survey (United States: Bureau of the Census, 1973a: VIII). The members of secondary families in 1970 were counted as secondary individuals in the household. The small numbers of secondary families for the contemporary period results from the almost total disappearance from the household of servants and lodgers who frequently composed a secondary family. While around 12 percent of the households for the sample period from 1850 to 1880 contained a secondary family, the percentage in 1970 would have been less than one-fifth of one percent. Hence, with only a few exceptions, every family had its own household.

Contemporary family size has declined since the 1850 to 1880 sample period by about one person. The decline is less than has been traditionally believed and less than the decline for household size over the same period. Also, while household size for both periods displays a rather continuous and gradual decline, the family size pattern for both period displays a fluctuating pattern. For the contemporary period, the average size increased slightly in 1960 from the 1950 figure; in 1970 it declined to a figure almost identical to the 1950 figure. The amount of change over the last three decades was very small, i.e., the largest change (between 1950 and 1960) was little more than one-tenth of a person (.11). Futhermore, the distribution by percentage for the different sizes pointed out the relative stability of family size for this period. As in the 1850 to 1880 period, family size varied less than household size and displayed a pattern of change that was quite different—the trend was to show an increase during the period rather than a consistent decline.

Much of the decline in family size from the sample period to the contemporary period resulted from the same factors that caused the decline in household size. The main difference is that the changing living arrangements of lodgers and servants had little effect upon family size because only related persons who shared the same household were counted for this statistic. Hence, the decline in family size was less than for household size, in part, because those lodgers and servants who set up their own separate household were only switching from secondary to primary family units.

GENERAL COMPOSITION

What about those individuals who are a part of the family of residence but not a part of the family head's family of procreation? Data on families containing individuals who added a generation to the head's family of procreation (extended families) are presented in Table 5.3. (Comparable data from published reports are not available for 1950.) As expected, the percentage of such families is very low but, as in the 1850 to 1880 sample, an increase ensues in the percentage of extended families. Although the change is rather small between 1960 and 1970, both of these percentages are higher than most of those reported for the 1850 to 1880 sample period. Hence, the percentage of extended families has remained low for both periods with the lowest percentages occurring during the nineteenth century.

Much of the same discussion applies to the data for the percentage of families containing an additional nuclear family unit which does not include the family head—a subfamily. These data, presented in Table 5.4, show that only a very small percentage of

Table 5.3: Families by Generational Composition: Percentage Restricted Versus Extended, 1960-1970

Year	Percentage	Restricted (one or two generations)	Extended (three or more generations)
1960	100.0	94.5	5.5
1970	100.0	92.8	7.2

Source: United States: Bureau of the Census (1955; 1963a:450; 1973a:207).

families contained a subfamily. (Comparable 1950 data are not available but, based upon information received from the Bureau of the Census, the percent of families containing one or more subfamilies would be around 5%). Like the extended family data, the results for the 1850 to 1880 sample and the contemporary period are very similar. In neither period has more than 5 percent of the families contained a subfamily. The figures for the contemporary period only slightly excede those figures for the 1850 to 1880 sample period. One variation worth noting is that the differences between extended families and those with subfamilies were less during the sample period than in the contemporary period. Because subfamilies almost always add a generation to the family unit, this suggests that a different pattern was operating in each period. Several factors present today, such as more available housing, more work opportunities for women, and more and various family assistance services and agencies, make it less likely that a nuclear family will have to or want to move into and share a household with another related nuclear

Table 5.4: Percentage of Families With and Without Subfamilies, 1960-1970

Year	Total	No Subfamilies	One Subfamily or More
1960	100.0	96.8	03.2
1970	100.0	97.6	02.4

Source: United States: Bureau of the Census (1963b:1-459; 1973a:237).

Table 5.5: Number of Marital Pairs per Family, 1950-1970

Year	Families	Number of Marital Pairs	Number of Marital Pairs per Family
1950	38,310,980	35,006,330	.91
1960	45,128,397	40,473,199	.90
1970	51,142,862	44,597,574	.87

Source: United States: Bureau of the Census (1963b:1-97; 1963b:1-459; 1973a:23, 225).

family unit. Now it is more common for these other relatives in the household to be single individuals for which the family is providing a residence.

The percentage of incidence for both of these indices is roughly the same for each period that data are presented. In addition, the direction of the change and, to some extent, its magnitude are not in line with traditional contentions.

MARITAL PAIRS

The number of marital pairs per family are presented in Table 5.5. A slight decline in the number of marital pairs per family occurs for the contemporary period. The figures for this period are higher than most of the figures for the 1850 to 1880 sample period, which indicates an increase in the number of marital pairs per household for the contemporary period. This is in opposition to and, in effect, challenges one of the presumed effects of industrialization and urbanization upon the family, i.e., individuals, especially women, should become more independent from marriage and family relationships resulting in the increasing disruption of these relations.

Table 5.6: Percentage of Families by Presence of Head-Spouse or Head Only, 1950-1970

Year	Percentage	Head-Spouse Families	Head only
1950	100.0	87.1	12.6
1960	100.0	87.8	12.2
1970	100.0	86.0	14.0

Source: United States: Bureau of the Census (1955:2A-31; 1963b: 1-465; 1973a:23).

Table 5.7: Sex of Family Head by Percentage: 1950-1970

Year	Families	Percentage Male Head	Percentage Female Head
1950	38,453,391	90.7	9.3
1960	45,128,397	90.7	9.3
1970	51,142,862	89.2	10.8

Source: United States: Bureau of the Census (1955:2A-31; 1963b:1-465; 1973a:23).

The data presented in Tables 5.6 and 5.7 exhibit essentially the same pattern as for marital pairs. In Table 5.6 the number of families not headed by a married couple shows a slight overall increase, but is still lower than the percentages reported for the nineteenth century sample. In fact, in every decade of the sample period more families were headed by a single person than was the case in any of the contemporary decades. Hence, the chances of both parents being present in the family unit have slightly increased for the contemporary period. Table 5.7 presents data on the percent of female-headed families. For these data, the differences between the two period are even less. But, a number of figures for the earlier period still exceed the contemporary figures; thus, the percentage of female-headed families was generally higher for the 1850 to 1880 sample period. The data in Table 5.5, 5.6 and 5.7, when compared to the nineteenth century data, display trends opposite to traditional expectations. In addition, differences were not very large either between or within the periods and this lack of change is a further challenge to the traditional perspective.

Despite their similarity, diverse factors affected these rates in each time period. For the 1850 to 1880 period, most broken marriages were due either to the death of one partner or, to a lesser extent, divorce. More importantly, the remarriage rate for the surviving or divorced persons from a marriage, particularly among older persons in the population, was much lower than today (Glick, 1957:68). Of course, the remarriage rate for widowed individuals has always been lower than for divorced individuals. In the contemporary period, divorce has increasingly predominated as a method for dissolving a marriage. This is particularly true during the initial years of marriage when a couple is usually involved with child rearing. This results from a lower mortality rate for the entire population (including certain segments of the older population) and changes in attitudes and laws concerning divorce and remarriage. The latter factor, in particular, contributed to an increasing divorce rate. Despite these changes for the contemporary period, the percentages in Tables 5.5, 5.6 and 5.7 indicate a slightly lower percentage of single parent families. This is due primarily to a much higher remarriage rate after widowhood and divorce. Hence, for the contemporary period, the percentage of couple-headed families was slightly higher; at the same time, however, the chances were less that this was the first marriage for the couple.

NUMBER OF CHILDREN

The final structural aspect considered is the number of children per family. Table 5.8 presents the number, percentage distribution, and measures of central tendency for the number of children per family. (The mean number of children for 1950 was not reported in the published summary reports utilized, and none of the reports provided enough information to allow the calculation of the mean.) For 1960 and 1970, the average number of children residing in a family was around 1.3 for children under eighteen and around 1.5 for all children regardless of age. (Based upon information supplied by the Bureau of the Census, the mean for children under eighteen in 1950 is estimated to be lower with a value of 1.15.) Since no distinction in children's ages was made for the nineteenth century sample period, the latter figure (1.5) should be the one compared to the earlier period. The overall difference between the two periods, then, is a little over one child per family. This difference is smaller than the traditional perspectives would suggest, but is still the most important for any of the family aspects studied. Like the trend for family size to which changes in this aspects are closely linked, the direction of change has not always been consistent with traditional expectations.

Two similarities for the statistics on children between the nineteenth century and contemporary periods seem worth

Table 5.8: Number and Percentage Distribution of Head's Own Children Under 18 per Family, 1950-1970

Number of Children	1950	1960	1970
All Units	38,453,391	45,128,305	51,142,862
Percentage	100.0	100.0	100.0
No children	48.4	43.1	44.8 $(34.4)^a$
1 child	21.0	18.4	18.0 $(22.4)^a$
2 children	16.5	18.0	17.0 $(19.4)^a$
3 children or more	14.2	20.5	20.1 $(23.7)^a$
Modal number	0.00	0.00	0.00
Median number	0.58	0.83	0.79 $(1.19)^a$
Mean number	$(1.15)^b$	1.34 $(1.54)^a$	1.30 $(1.54)^a$

Source: United States: Bureau of the Census (1955:2A-19; 1963a:21; 1963b:1-463; 1973a:23, 39, 213); Glick (1957:39).

a. These higher figures result from the inclusion of all children of the head regardless of age who live in the same household. These higher figures are the ones compared with the 1800s data as these data included all children in the household regardless of age.

b. Figure taken from Glick (1957:39) and based upon data from Current Population Reports for 1953.

mentioning. First, with the exception of one decade, the mean (as well as the median) figures for each census throughout each period were nearly alike. Second, the decade for which the figures were the exception occurred at an unexpected time. For the sample period the mean number of children dipped rather sharply in 1870 but was followed in 1880 by an increase. This resulted in a figure very similar to the means for the first two decades. For the contemporary period the first decade (1950) provided a much lower figure relative to 1960 and 1970. The distributions in Table 5.8 show why this was the case. The percentage of families with no children was at its highest level in 1950—5 percent higher than the 1960 figure. On the other end of the distribution, the percentage of families with three or more children was at its lowest level for the 1950 census. This was about 6 percent below the figures for both the 1960 and 1970 censuses. As with the nineteenth century data, involvement in war emerges as a factor in explaining the change that had taken place. Prior to the 1940s, the birth rates and completed fertility rates had reached their lowest point ever (Coale and Zelnik, 1963). During the 1940s, overall these rates increased with the exception of those years in which the United States was involved in World War II. After this involvement was terminated, both the birth rate and total fertility rate shot up sharply. During the 1950s, the birth rate leveled off but was still at a much higher level than before. The completed fertility level continued to climb. This resulted in what has been termed the "postwar baby boom." The effect of this boom upon the number of children per family was only beginning to be felt in the 1950 census because many of the families enumerated had born their children during those years when the fertility and birth rates were much lower. The families that would contribute to the "baby boom" had just been formed and the majority of their children were yet to be born. It was not until 1960, that the full effect of the "baby boom" was realized in terms of the number of children residing in the family at the time of the census enumeration. Because the birth rate leveled off at a higher level while the fertility rate continued to climb a bit longer before it leveled off, the 1970 data remained at a level almost identical to the 1960 figures.

Beside the obviously important role of fertility and birth rates in determining the number of children per family, additional factors are responsible for some of the changes that occurred in these figures. For example, the percentage of families having either one child or two children was quite similar for both the nineteenth century sample and the contemporary period. The biggest variation between the two periods occurred for the percentage of families having no children. The percentages for the contemporary period are, on the average, more than double the figures for the sample period. This difference is only to a limited extent due to the lower fertility and birth rates in the contemporary period or to the percentage of couples who never had any children. Most of the increase results from a combination of several related variables. In the contemporary family due to changes in mortality the chances are better for the joint survival of a couple after their children leave home. In addition, when only one parent survives the likelihood has increased that this person will remarry. The availability of more housing units and more opportunities for financial independence means the chances are better today that these couples will be able to maintain a residence separate from their children. For the families which have children present, the biggest change has been the disappearance of families containing a large number of children.

Typical Family Structure, 1950-1970

As the various family aspects have been presented for the contemporary period, it has become clear that the structure of the family has changed little throughout these three decades. In addition the incidence of most of these structural aspects are fairly similar to the ones reported for the 1850 to 1880 sample. The biggest variation is in the number of children residing in the family, which also accounts for most of the change in family size. These two characteristics, then, are responsible for most of the change in the structure of the American family since 1850. These changes, which are small, and the lack of change in the other areas refute the traditionally held view that industrialization and urbanization created dramatic changes in family structure.

The data for the contemporary period suggest a family unit that typically consisted of a nuclear unit, which was in most cases the family of procreation for the family head. The family consisted of a married couple, one of whom was designated the head, with the only other members present, if any, being children of the couple. When children were present, usually only one or two resided with the family. No additional relatives were present outside this nuclear unit. This description would apply to the vast majority of families in each of the contemporary decades—1950 to 1970.

As was expected, only a very small percentage (less than 10 percent) of the families included relatives outside of the head's family of procreation. Just as with the nineteenth century family data, when other relatives were present, these individuals were in most cases the parents or parent of either the husband or wife who headed the family. One difference was that during the sample period, the parents tended to be those of the husband, while today the parents tended to be those of the wife. Like before, the presence of other relatives other than parents was even less in evidence.

Hence, the typical family for the contemporary period was quite similar to the one presented for the nineteenth century. The biggest variation took place in the number of children residing in the household at the time of the census. For the contemporary family the chances were much higher that no children would reside with the family or couple. To some extent this change is misleading because most of the alteration in the percentage of families with no children was due to changes that occurred for the older members of the population. Increases in the joint survival of parents after their children left home and much higher remarriage rates for this same group when divorce from or death of a spouse does occur, added considerably to the percentage of families with no children residing in the household during the contemporary period.

Just as with the 1850 to 1880 sample data, the amount of change in the various family aspects was relatively small for the contemporary period. Most of the mean scores or percentages for the aspects varied very little throughout the period. In this case the small amount of variation was expected based upon the presumed stability of the family during a post industrial period. The fact that these aspects also did not vary much more during the sample period suggests the historical stability of family structure.

In contrast, household size displayed the greatest and most consistent variance for the contemporary period. The decline in household size seems to be a continuation of the decrease displayed during the sample period. As noted in Chapter 3, household size was the only aspect that completely followed the expected pattern of change—a decline in the incidence of the phenomena for each decade. Ironically, it was during the contemporary period that several family aspects in addition to household size followed this expected pattern, i.e., the percentage of families with subfamilies, the number of marital pairs in the family, and the number of male-headed households. In addition, where only three out of the eight aspects showed an overall decline in incidence for the sample period, five of the eight aspects showed an overall decline for the contemporary period. This suggests that the traditional view of family change might have been based upon and supported by the occurrences (changes) that have happened over the last several decades. Regardless of how appropriate this view is for the contemporary period, it clearly does not apply to data from the nineteenth century and earlier. The data presented in this chapter as they are compared to earlier data certainly provide the grounds (or at least a reason) for a reexamination of our traditional conceptions of family change and suggest the necessity of supporting this effort with historical family research.

In conclusion it is clear that structurally the family has varied very little during the contemporary period. In addition, the structural characteristics that are appropriate for the contemporary family are quite similar to the structural aspects found to apply to earlier American families.

Chapter 6

QUANTITATIVE SOCIAL HISTORIES

This Study and Beyond

The purpose of this work has been twofold. First, the attempt has been made to present the most complete and up-to-date historical description of the American family's structure. Second, this study has attempted to explore in more detail and test one of the most popular explanations of family change—the role of industrialization and urbanization.

Various sources were used to provide as complete a description of American family structure as possible at this time. But a lot of gaps still exist in the data, both in terms of missing time periods as well as in a lack of representativeness. Despite these gaps it is possible to present a general historical picture of the American family for a number of different structural aspects. Comparable data on most of the structural aspects considered have been compiled and presented for each century from the American colonial period to the present. Additional figures on some of these aspects are available but the emphasis has been upon presenting data that would be reasonably comparable to data from other periods.

Summary of Findings for Study

What can be stated about the history of American family structure in general based upon the data presented? The general pattern seems to be one of relative stability. There is no doubt that some of the structural aspects of the family have changed. In most cases, however, the change has been much less than traditionally presumed and has not always gone in the expected direction. The observed structural aspect that has gone through the greatest amount of change is not really a family characteristic at all—it is household size. This aspect is usually considered synonymous with family size because most of today's households consist only of members from the same family unit. But even in the nineteenth century, the U.S. Bureau of the Census failed to make a distinction between these two aspects. Household size in its relationship to family size has made a major shift over the periods studied. In the colonial period and in the nineteenth century, average household size was always larger than average family size by about one-half person or more, while for the contemporary period average household size is usually about one-half person less than average family size. Prior to the twentieth century, households tended to include resident employees and lodgers in addition to primary family members. Frequently a number of these residents were related to one another and constituted a secondary family unit. Today this practice has almost disappeared. At the same time a continued increase in the number of single person households has made it possible for the average household size to be lower than the average family size. Although the change in family size has not been as large as the one for household size, it has declined throughout the period studied.

Another structural aspect whose decline is almost equal to that of family size and primarily responsible for its decline, is the number of children residing in the family. The fact that the changes in the number of children per family accounts for most of the change in family size indicates the lack of change in the other structural aspects that would also have affected family size.

Further historical study on fertility and child rearing patterns of the American family should tell us much more about this important historical change in American family structure.

The remaining family aspects have changed even less since the American colonial period. Data on the generational composition of the family leave little doubt that the nuclear family unit has been the predominant pattern for every time period observed. During each period the vast majority of families (usually over 90 percent) followed this pattern, and only a very small minority of families were ever either vertically or horizontally extended. When the family was extended, the most likely pattern was for it to be extended generationally (vertically) while horizontal extension was virtually nonexistent. The nineteenth century data seem to support the idea that an extended family of residence is most frequently a temporary arrangement providing aid and services and is usually based upon economic considerations. During the nineteenth century there were two different periods during the family life cycle in which an extended family of residence was the most likely to occur. When couples were first married, some tended to reside temporarily with one of their parents. The other period was when the parents of a married couple who had had a separate household were no longer able to maintain their own households or their spouse had died. As a result they often moved into the home of one of their offspring. More families experienced an extended situation sometime during their life cycle than these statistics indicate (cf., Berkner, 1972), however, it still was the exception and not the rule. The characteristics of the additional nuclear families (subfamilies) beyond the head's nuclear unit in the nineteenth century sample suggest that the latter was providing aid and services to these other relatives. These subfamilies tended to be broken families and, in many cases, displayed the structure of a single parent family with one or more children. For the contemporary family all of these patterns still exist; however, there have been some changes. Newly married couples are less prone to share, even on a temporary basis, the household of either of their parents. On the other hand, due primarily to changes in the mortality rate, there actually has been an increase of families that include parents of the head or the head's spouse. The nineteenth century pattern for subfamilies still continues, and seems particularly appropriate for younger families where the husband's occupation demands frequent and long absences, such as military service. In addition, divorce has become more important than mortality in the contemporary period as a basis for creating a broken family.

The lack of change for the marital pairs, the couple-headed families, and the sex of family head data also suggest the stability of the family in these areas historically. Hence, the appropriate historical image of the American family structure is one of stability. Most of the change that has occurred has resulted from the reduction in the number of children residing in the family.

The second endeavor of this work was to study the popular contention that industrialization and urbanization as a part of modernization brought about important changes in the American family. As suggested earlier, the use of the industrialization and urbanization processes by many observers to explain familial as well as other societal change, has almost bordered upon being an article of faith. The major question raised was how close this contention is to social reality.

In the past, many historical observations about the American family have been based upon an uncritical and unsystematic use of various literary sources. Often the personal observations of famous contemporary figures were relied upon the heaviest. As a result the most wealthy and influential families were the ones most frequently portrayed. These families were, of course, atypical. There are, obviously, major difficulties in generalizing about American families from various levels of society when knowledge is based only upon family patterns representative of a small atypical segment. The family data selected for presentation in this study not only had to be historically comparable but also had to be as representative as possible for all segments of the American population regardless of social or economic level. The colonial data have some serious geographical limitations, but the family data presented for the various colonial communities are based upon all of the community's population and not just the social and economic elite. For the latter half of the nineteenth century with the availability of the original manuscript census schedules for the entire United States population, the data are by no means limited to an atypical group of American families. These census schedules provide a basis for the reconstruction of individual family units representing wide cross-sections of American society. Families from the very bottom of the socioeconomic level of American society up to and including the top level can be studied. For the contemporary period the data reported by the U.S. Bureau of the Census were utilized. These data based upon extremely large and clearly representative samples include all segments of the society.

The historical descriptive data themselves provide a very general test of the effects of industrialization and urbanization upon family structure. Certainly, the presumed dramatic effects that these processes were to have had upon the family never occurred. This was due to the fact that the family structural aspects expected to precede the development of industrialization and urbanization never were present to any great extent. The suggestion that these processes either brought about or demanded a nuclear family unit seems completely unsound. Although not always due to the same set of circumstances, without doubt, the nuclear family of residence has always been and continues to be the predominant type of family. The descriptive data provide other challenges to the presumed effects of industrialization and urbanization because the incidence of certain family patterns increased when they were expected to decline. For example, the 1850 to 1880 sample period was one of intense and rapid industrialization and urbanization. During this period the percentage of extended families and families with subfamilies was actually increasing. In addition, the incidence of these family patterns was lower in the beginning of the nineteenth century sample period than in the contemporary period. The trend was much the same for the number of marital pairs in the family and the number of families headed by a married couple. Instead of declining, the patterns showed an increase during the nineteenth century sample period. Furthermore, the incidence of these patterns was generally lower during the sample period than during the contemporary period. This is the reverse of what has traditionally been expected. The percentage of families headed by females was also generally higher in the nineteenth century sample period. Although none of these patterns varied very much in the incidence, it cannot be ignored that the change which did occur was contrary to what was presumed to take place. The number of children per family and family size have a rather direct relationship to one another and remain as the two aspects which changed (declined) overall in the direction expected. However, this decline was much smaller than expected, and the patterns for these aspects did fluctuate in that several decades registered increases in their incidences.

The nineteenth century sample in addition to providing descriptive data also permitted a more direct test of the effects of industrialization and urbanization upon the family. It was possible to place each sample family in a particular type of industrialized-urbanized environment using a number of indices that were either a measure of or a part of these two processes. The results challenge the presumed effects of these two processes upon the family. The amount of variance in the family structural aspects explained by the industrialization and urbanization variables varied from a low to an almost nonexistent level. It was, in fact, household size that showed the strongest relationship. As suggested by the descriptive family structural data, family size and the number of children per family had the strongest relationship to the independent variables. This relationship was far from strong but appears "strong" in comparison to the nearly nonexistent association found for the other family aspects. Of course, these results were not surprising in light of the lack of change in the structure of the families throughout the sample period.

Historically, then, it seems that the family has maintained a high level of structural integrity. At any point in time, the make-up of the majority of families has been essentially identical. The role of external pressures upon the family unit apparently has been minimal. Only a very small proportion of family units have been involved in most of the structural change noted here. The processes of industrialization and urbanization evidently have played only a very minor role in family change. Other studies (B. Laslett, 1973) have suggested that any limited set of external forces by themselves would probably play the same minor role in family change. Too much emphasis can be placed upon the family's structural integrity, however. One phenomena that has helped maintain this integrity has been the existence of offsetting factors in various periods. For example, in the preindustrial period the expectation of a large, extended family might have stimulated activity capable of attaining such an end. But certain demographic (e.g., infant mortality and shorter life expectancy) and economic (e.g., family wealth and size of living quarters) factors all but made realization of this expectation impossible. On the other hand, with the improved standard of living and postponed mortality, a large, extended family would be much easier to realize today, but the expectations are such that few individuals choose to follow this option. In fact, today those individuals who can least afford it are more inclined to have larger and extended families. Thus, internal factors like personal choice are more important and influential today. If this argument is pursued too vigorously, however, the indication is much the same as the one for the traditional perspective described in Chapter 1, i.e., the behavior of the family is at the mercy of external forces, especially during the preindustrial period. Some evidence, though, suggests that family members engaged in behavior which limited families' size (Wrigley, 1966a) and limited their association and relationships with kin (Anderson, 1971) even during the preindustrial period. Hence, to some degree this structural integrity of the family was maintained historically as a result of family membership decisions.

If historically the family has maintained its structural integrity, some of our ideas about "modern life" must be questioned. Supposedly, it was the processes of industrialization and urbanization which brought about the small, mobile, and independent family. A part of this change was an increasing emphasis upon equality between the sexes for both children and adults. Both the authority of the husband over his wife and the authority of parents over their children are thought to have declined. The family has become an institution that primarily provides emotional solace to members who are increasingly more independent of its authority. As a result the family unit has become much more fragile and fragmented. This, in turn, has had an important impact upon the behavior of individual family members. In fact, many observers have attributed the individual activity that has led to much of the social and personal disorganization in "modern life" to the changes in the family brought about by industrialization and urbanization. This study, however, suggests that at least in the United States the typical family has always been small, mobile, and independent. Hence, the widely accepted argument used to explain modern society's ills is challenged. The role of industrialization and urbanization in causing these ills has possibly been exaggerated just as it has in the case of family change.

Why, then, does this traditional explanation for both family change and society's ills persist? One answer might be that it is a view of history that seems to be passed down from one generation to the next. Each new generation tends to see social patterns as changing recently and rapidly. In support of this, the social patterns of the previous generation are characterized as being essentially unchanged from many prior generations. The practice of lamenting the swiftness of contemporary change and its resulting ills in contrast to the more "stable and harmonious" social patterns of the past is old and deeply engrained. This practice persists in spite of evidence to the contrary. One reason may be that it provides an easily identifiable and more acceptable explanation of the present state of society by providing a basis for a stark comparison. At the same time, this practice tends to be used as a justification for traditional customs and behavior by those desiring a return to "harmony and stability." Finally, there seems to be a certain satisfaction gained by many from an idealization of the past.

Another element contributing to an acceptance of the traditional view of social change has been the shrinking of the world in which we live. As a result of advances in communication and transportation we have become more aware of the ills of our own society as well as those of other societies throughout the world. Related to this are certain value changes (see Chapter 1) that have brought about a rise in our expectations concerning family life and life in general. These factors have led to an emphasis upon the ills of contemporary life and support the idea of recent rapid change while, at the same time, they ironically increase the need for a nostalgic look at the past. All of these elements, in turn, support the traditional view of family change.

Despite this justification of the traditional view the data presented in this study suggest that the processes of industrialization or urbanization do not determine the shape of the family, or vice versa—although these processes and family structure do have some influence upon one another. An example is the role the family has played as a catalyst in the industrialization of some societies where characteristics of the family system at a minimum facilitated industrial growth (cf., Goode, 1964:114-116).

In summary, the data presented in this study provide a basis for a clearer understanding of the American family as it has existed historically. In addition, the data challenge the traditional contention concerning the dramatic effects of industrialization and urbanization upon the structure of the family. Support for the latter conclusion can be found in a recent review of work dealing with the history of the American family (Adams, 1975: 51-80). Even if our attention is focused upon what has changed historically in the family only "a few of these developments can be directly related to the industrial revolution (p. 79)." Despite all the emphasis upon the role of industrialization it turns out to be "extremely difficult" to establish "direct linkages between the family and industrialization."

Limitations and Contributions:
This Work and the General Approach

There are important limitations to this work, and as in most research more questions are raised than are really answered. In a very real sense little has been positively proven. More precisely, the available evidence has been presented and reviewed with the result that certain perspectives and explanations of family change seem appropriate.

As the evidence is derived from the census and other similar documents, a number of limitations are important and inescapable. Although family units can be reconstructed from parish records, family wills, and manuscript census schedules, life cannot be breathed into these families. The use of these records has been widespread over the last couple of decades primarily because these are the most accessible data and are of a quantitative nature. The data do allow the structural reconstruction of family units and can be the basis for inferences about other family aspects but the outcome is far from the total picture necessary to completely understand family history. It is clear that other sources must be used to complement these data.

But even census data with their accessibility, quantitative nature, and wide range must be used cautiously. One must rely upon the established definitions and procedures plus the application of both of these by those who initially recorded the data. Berkner (1975) in a review of Laslett and Wall's (1972) book, *Household and Family in Past Time,* did an excellent job of pointing out the weaknesses of census type data. The problems include incomplete data (e.g., the ages of individuals not provided), it being unclear how enumerators determined "blocks" (households) of individuals, and the purpose of the census, which affects how and what is recorded (pp. 724-727). He argued that when one tries to determine household and family units regardless of the census definition, a whole range of variables must be considered including the following: common consumption, common production, residential closeness of kin, settlement patterns, and architectural forms. In general, household structure "must be derived from the context of the society in which it is found" (p.727). He concluded that census data are no more "hard" data than many other sources and are "just as likely to be 'lying'" (p. 725).

Fortunately, several of Berkner's criticisms are not appropriate for the census data used here. The missing data examples he cited are available from most the censuses utilized. Thanks to the work that has been done on the U.S. census and especially Wright's (1900) book we have some clear indicatioins as to how "blocks" of individuals were determined for most of the censuses. Finally, the purpose of the U.S. censuses have been relatively consistent throughout their history. Wright's book even provided some insight into the individual decisions and interpretations made by the census marshalls. However, it is correct that definitions, procedures, and applications did vary somewhat for each census and across time. In addition, these problems are, to some extent, compounded by the codings and inferences made when the data are utilized at a later time. A good deal of caution is necessary when using census type data, and in this study every attempt has been made to present data which are comparable.

The data and discussion in this study relate primarily to the structural aspects of the family of residence. What about the structure of the family of interaction and the behavior patterns for both the family of residence and interaction? This question points out the rather limited view of this study; however, the most accessible and available data tended to define this study's focus. Obviously these other areas must be studied and reviewed to complement the results.

It is essential that further efforts be made, particularly in the area of family behavior patterns. The reconstruction of behavior patterns for the family historically is going to be much more difficult than that for the structural aspects. These patterns lend themselves less to quantification, they were less frequently recorded, and the primary sources that must be utilized are extant literary sources, whose limitations were noted in Chapter 2. Recent research has made it evident that these sources, particularly diaries, are of very little value in providing quantitative data about the family. But the systematic use of several different types of verbal data sources can provide important information on structure and especially behavior patterns including characterizing relationships in the family, beliefs systems, and attitudes.

Some recent work on the history of the family has demonstrated the utility and significance of literary sources when used systematically. One example is the work on family structure in nineteenth century Lancashire, England completed by Anderson (1971). He used verbal data—abstracting descriptive material from contemporary sources—to supplement and support his quantitative data, which were mostly nineteenth century census data. Descriptive material from a wide variety of sources was used, including contemporary books, articles, newspapers, Parliamentary papers and debates, and letters (pp. 181-194). An effort (p. 180) was made to handle the data in such a way as to reduce premature conclusions and to establish the typical patterns based only upon an overall balance of evidence. Although this method might, by some standards, lack precision, the resulting work is a good example of the complementary use of both quantitative and qualitative data. Another excellent example was provided by Edward Shorter's (1975) work on the rise of the "modern" family. Shorter is very much aware of the limitations for certain types of verbal data even though they can provide entertaining anecdotes which make the reading of history a more enjoyable pastime. Consequently, he decided to essentially ignore most "literary sources" (which he defined as novels and the other writings of "cultivated pens") because of their class bias and lack of representativeness (p. 9). Instead he wanted to use the writings of observers who had "preserved accounts of lives other than their own for posterity" (p. 11). This led him to utilize observations made by local medical doctors, minor bureaucrats, antiquarians, and folklorists. These sources were considered by Shorter to be " a compromise between the narrowness of quantitative analysis and the possibly atypical descriptions of concrete places in fixed times" (p. 10). The result was a much richer and more complete historical portrayal of the family. The final example is the work carried out by Lantz et al. (1968; 1973; 1975; 1977) which relied primarily upon one literary source—magazines—to provide a history of the American family from 1741 to 1865. Through a systematic content analysis of these magazines much information was gathered on family behavior that otherwise is difficult to obtain (e.g., power relationships between husband and wife, role of romantic love in mate selection, motivations for marriage, sanctions for sexual deviance, and conflict between parents and between parents and children). In several cases, the material in the magazines vividly presented the existence of family patterns which were contrary to the commonly postulated patterns for a preindustrial society. Lantz et al. (1977:421) concluded that it is a "possibility that literary sources, such as magazines, reflected the early signs of family change in America." These then are some excellent examples of works using verbal data that focus primarily upon behavior patterns (except Anderson) of the family. Despite their contributions and care in data utilization, they have come under attack. Some of these criticisms will be considered later.

The study of these behavior patterns is, indeed, important because many are presumed to have changed over time. This has even become more crucial over the last two decades as more and more work has noted the lack of change in regard to structural characteristics of the family. Again, the processes of industrialization and urbanization as part of modernization are emphasized as the active agents bringing about this change. But even if the focus is only on behavior patterns of the family, little evidence exists to support the presumed role of these "active" agents in family change (cf., Adams, 1975; Anderson, 1971; Lantz et al., 1977; Shorter, 1975). Two things become increasingly clear, family change was much less dramatic during industrial and urban development than we have assumed in the past and many of the presumed changes brought on by these two developments occurred prior to their initiation. It will be difficult to achieve a total historical documentation of these behavior patterns. Nevertheless, this step is necessary if we are to have a complete understanding of how and why these behavior patterns have changed.

Even the available data documenting the structural aspects of the American family over the last four centuries have many time-period gaps. Some comparable family structural data for each of these centuries are now available, but much more data in terms of time periods and types are needed before the complete picture is known. Also, important "geographical gaps" still exist. This is especially true for the colonial period where the data presented are primarily derived from one particular geographical area—

the New England colonies. Related to this is the almost complete lack of data for family life in and on the American frontier. This is particularly sad in light of the importance often accorded the frontier in bringing about changes in the family (Lantz and Snyder, 1969:37-50).

The selection of the measures for industrialization and urbanization used in this study was also based primarily upon their availability. It is not claimed that these variables are necessarily either the best or the only measures able to represent either of these processes. In fact, it is imperative that this study's analysis should be seen primarily as an initial attempt to aid in the further consideration and testing of the relationship between the family and the processes of industrialization and urbanization. In defense of the measures, it should be added that there is little doubt that these indices are a part of or at least a result of these processes.

Some of the recent work on the social history of the family, particularly that work which has emphasized a quantitative approach, has come under much criticism. These criticisms, while not leveled at this study, are directed at the type of approach this work takes. Hence, a general discussion of both the limits and uses of quantitative techniques and work is appropriate. [For other discussions, see Aydelotte et al. (1972); Berkner (1975); Forster (1974); and Lasch (1975a; 1975b; 1975c).] Most of the uses or advantages of historical quantitative research can be grouped into five different areas—finding patterns (both uniformities and deviations); handling large volumes of data; dealing with broad issues; suggesting further research; and providing baselines. Relevant criticisms will be dealt with as each of these areas are addressed.

A clearly demonstrated use of this research is to find and establish the *existence of patterns* in the data being studied. This can result from simply summarizing the data by providing a frequency distribution and/or measures of central tendency. Examples of this are presented in Chapters 2 and 3. The information organized in this way can be used to establish patterns, indicate the absence of any pattern, or show the various paths of departures from the norm. In many cases even more sophisticated measures (e.g., indices) which establish different levels or degrees of a phenomena can be developed, thus going beyond the mere indication of either the presence or absence of the phemonena. As the application of multiple regression in Chapter 4 shows, very powerful instruments of statistical analysis can be applied which, in turn, enable the researcher to test formulated hypotheses rather quickly. Even the use of statistical inference is a very real possibility, which will allow a smaller group of elements (sample) to represent a large population.

At the same time, as critics have noted, some persistent limitations must be kept in mind. As the researcher is relying upon previously collected data (of course, this is true for all historical research), it is imperative that he know from whom the data were collected; why, how, and by whom it was gathered; and the definitions of terms applied. As Berkner (1975:726-727) noted even what may appear to be an elementary concept (e.g., household) may vary significantly over time and space in its application by data-gathering agencies. This is demonstrated by the changes that have occurred in the definition of the family as applied by the Census Bureau in the United States. Another problem limited primarily to census type sources is that the data tend to be cross-sectional in nature. Hence, these sources are of limited utility if the issue in question relates to the various processes that are a part of family life. As several critics have observed, especially Berkner (1975:729-731), the so-called differences in family structure that have been presented by many observers may, in fact, be merely the representation of different phases in the family life cycle. Relying upon cross-sectional data fails to answer this question unless certain controls are introduced, such as the age of household/family heads, which is not always available. Problems may also arise when one compares data for the same place in time but from different types of sources. An example is the disagreement in the colonial American family literature about the structure of the family—was it a modified extended or nuclear unit (see Chapter 2)? The disagreements turn out to be the consequence of two problems already mentioned—application of definitions (one group defined the family in terms of interaction, while the other in terms of residence) and type of data (one group used a cross-sectional source, which counted only family members alive and present in the household at one point in time, while the other used a longitudinal source, which counted the completed family unit regardless of residence or length of life). A problem which may plague information that is not already quantified is the forcing of unique and sometimes very diverse cases into one category or group. For example, when many researchers simply dichotomize family structure into two groups—extended versus nuclear—a wide variety of situations are grouped together in each category. Even in the simplest of the two groups—nuclear family units—in addition to a unit composed of a married couple and their children, the following would also qualify as nuclear units in most research: a married couple; a single parent and child(ren); and two siblings. The categorization of data is necessary to establish uniformities; one cannot, however, avoid the problem of losing some of the uniques of the data. Hence, the establishment of categories is a very crucial decision that is all too often taken lightly. A final criticism is that the search for uniformities leads us away from questions of cultural values and emotional qualities in human relationship because these are virtually impossible to quantify. This is easily demonstrated by much of the recent work on the social history of the family (however, this does not have to be the case, as the discussion below on providing baselines will indicate). Overall, despite the important problems noted by critics, the quantification approach has been and can be very useful in the face of varied and confusing data. It can show where we stand on a given problem by providing the following: extent of uniformities, significance of exceptions, qualifications required of generalizations related to the problem, and a basis for confidence in the findings.

An implied point in the above discussion is that the techniques employed to search for uniformities permit researchers to deal with *large amounts of data*. These techniques permit easy control over large volumes of data that would otherwise be difficult if not totally impossible to handle. In other words, these techniques grant access to, and exploitation of, reservoirs of important historical data that traditional historical "research techniques" would have great difficulty in managing effectively. It is possible to work with manuscript census schedules and deal with a large sample (over 10,000 cases in this study) of the population which represents all of its segments. A great advantage in this case is that the researcher can go beyond the elite of the population to get a more encompassing image because he has data on the majority of the individuals in the population who left virtually no written record.

The criticisms mentioned before are also relevant here and are essential for the researcher to keep in mind when carrying out a project. One additional point concerning the scope of the research needs to be made. In contrast to this emphasis upon volumes and large amounts of data, the scope of the research is (and should) not be too wide. The vast majority of the literature reports on research which is rather limited both in terms of time and space. Part of this is due to an attempt to reduce some of the difficulties associated with the use of available data as noted earlier. Whatever the reason for the limited scope, several critics argue that the outcome is a great deal of information about "nothing." On the other hand, Aydelotte et al. (1972:9) argued that a restricted focus may be the "principal merit" of the quantitative approach for a number of reasons. It permits the researcher to take more advantage of selected parts of the data. We can utilize more fully the data which can be more strictly manipulated by means of statistical analysis. The result is having the data subjected to more refined analysis, which increases the precision of the research findings. Thus, in this research an important trade-off exists—to increase precision, the scope must to some extent be reduced.

This takes us into the next area—the ability of this type of research to *deal with broad issues*. The concern with precision could be interpreted as producing very thorough and rigorous but trivial research. But quite the contrary point is made by those who argue for the use of quantification. They suggest that some broad historical problems which previously have only been dealt with in rather general terms can now be treated more effectively. The precision of the evidence gathered using this approach can often be the basis for moving closer to a solution for some of these problems. In some cases, the findings may be the only tangible evidence available, and even though only indirectly related to a problem, can be grounds for what Aydelottes (p. 4) calls "inductive inferences." For example, Smith's (1973a) demographic analysis of the marriage patterns for the sons and daughters of colonial American families provided hard data, which suggested a great deal about the decline of parental authority (see Chapter 2). The primary alternative to his data offered by earlier work was historical speculation. This is only one example among many available of these techniques contributing to a better understanding of important and broad historical issues in the family. But despite this potential, much of the completed research has ignored family behavior and norms. To some extent, this is a result of the emphasis upon and in some cases the exclusive use of census type data. The implied assumption by some researchers in these cases is that census data do not lie while verbal sources do [see Berkner's (1975:724) critique of Laslett and Wall (1972)]. However, an honest evaluation of census data raises questions about their validity which the researcher must be aware of. Keeping in mind the difficulties, even so-called trivial points—because they are based upon a systematic application of techniques—may have important implications for much larger issues. The consequences may include new insights, a reformulation of the problem, and, at a minimum, an advance in the discussion of the problem.

These results relate to the next area—*suggesting further research*—which is often an unexpected consequence of work using quantification techniques. Frequently, in the literature it is noted that the research has provided an unanticipated pattern for a relationship which calls for explanation. As exhibited in Chapters 3 and 4 the patterns in some of the data repeatedly implied the dramatic effects that the Civil War had upon the family. This, then, becomes a concern for further research. One problem as noted by critics which has probably reduced the acceptance level of findings from the quantitative histories has been the failure of researchers to elaborate upon the techniques being applied. As many of these techniques and related arguments are of recent origin or application, it is necessary to spell them out more than would be the case in most other areas of research. The elaboration of techniques and arguments should be instructive, suggestive, and provide the reader with a better basis on which to make an evaluation.

The final use area is the ability of this research to *provide baselines* both in terms of specific statistical indices that enable the quantitative measure of change and in a broader sense by contributing to more complete and accurate portraits of past family life styles. The discussion for all the previous areas suggests this use of quantitative research in providing both types of historical baselines. In addition, the various criticisms noted must be dealt with. In carrying out this type of research, it is important that one keeps in mind what the overriding goal should be. It is not the acquisition of a complete knowledge of past reality but more realistically an increasingly closer approximation of it. Many of the criticisms directed at this approach result from the assumption that the former is the goal of this research, and critical remarks imply that quantitative social histories "should" produce indisputable findings, complete explanations, and even universal laws. A close reading of the research reports available connotes just the opposite. To the author's knowledge, nobody claims that his results are conclusive or final. Quite the contrary, many authors are aware of their works' limitations and appropriately qualify their findings. Most researchers realize that statistical manipulation merely rearranges the data. Regardless of how accurate the computations are, this "by no means betokens a similar precision of knowledge regarding the substantive matters" (Aydelottes et al., 1972:10). These techniques of analysis can only be as useful as the evidence permits. If the data lack validity and reliability, no conclusions of any kind can be drawn. Further, even if we have the most valid and reliable data available, the results would rarely exhibit a single pattern or go in only one direction and, consequently, inhibit conclusive results. It also turns out that no matter how wide the scope of the quantitative data available, in the end traditional methods of historical research must be utilized. When it gets down to interpreting the "hard data," one must depend upon impressions, logic, and persuasion which are all part of what historians term imaginative sympathy. It is imperative though to keep in mind the initial point—the quality of the data. The theoretical argument must never take priority over the quality of the data. The result could be quantitative data that are either unrelated or so indirectly related to the research problem that the interpretation is, in fact, merely speculation. This is a critical issue when using demographic data to study the family. This study's data tell us much about the formal structure of households but very little about emotional relations within the family. Hence, interpretations concerning the latter must be the result of very careful and cautious procedures.

Several related issues were raised by Lasch (1975a; 1975b; 1975c) in his strong attack on much of the recent work on the social history of the family. If one looks carefully, he did admit to the existence of "perfected useful techniques" (1975c:53) and the need for more empirical studies (1975a:37), but his main thrust was that the research results in this area have been very disappointing. The problem as he saw it was a consequence of the inattention given to theory. He contended that the findings are virtually meaningless because the theories and concepts that have been utilized are too crude, dated, and rigid. For example, he cited the use of ideal typologies inherited from the founders of sociology. The modernization theory which Lasch claimed has been the basis for most of this research is merely a slightly altered update of these earlier typologies. The outcome has been that most of the research taken together has tended to focus primarily on a rather limited set of concerns which has stifled the growth of this area. Lasch attributed this to the theoretical perspective which has dominated this research. Hence, the theoretical assumptions associated with the modernization perspective

all the more if implicit and unexamined, determine the selection
and interpretation of facts, and instead of guiding empirical work,
tyrannize over it, dictating in advance the outcome of investiga-
tions that ostensibly aim to uncover new facts (p. 37).

This work, which certainly has several of the faults noted by
critics, can be considered not only pertinent but as a partial
response to Lasch's main concern. In contrast to most work in
this area, it explicitly tries to test the effect of modernization
upon the family in several different ways (Chapter 3 and 4). It not
only indicates a lack of change in family structure [like Laslett
and Wall (1972) but for many more aspects] as a test of modernization theory but tries to measure several indices of the processes
underlying modernization—industrialization and urbanization—and their effect upon family structure. The result is no
support at all for the theory of modernization. This study's
findings like Laslett's essentially provide evidence in support of
Levy's arguments, which are spelled out in Chapter 1. Lasch is
partly correct when he suggests that "Laslett and his coworkers
[including this work] have succeeded only in establishing the
unimportance of the question to which they have devoted most of
their attention" (1975a:38). Nevertheless, work in this area
clearly has made several important contributions (the discussion
of uses above should suggest some of these) the last of which
strongly supports Lasch's main concern. First it adds detail to the
historical descriptions of early family systems. Historical research
does not study the past but only the "residues of the past which
have survived into the present" (Stedman Jones, 1976). Hence,
these quantitative techniques enable us to utilize some of the most
useful and complete (in terms of representing all of a population)
"residues" available. Second, even if it is conclusively shown that
family structure is not a useful variable in understanding historical change, it is a relationship which had to be tested. At a
minimum, it tells us what not to study in the future. Also it is
ridiculous to argue, as Lasch appears to suggest, that the only
worthwhile research takes place where dramatic differences are
discovered. As noted earlier, a lot of arguments and research

have suffered as a consequence of assuming the ubiquity of change. Finally, this work plainly indicates the need for both theoretical criticism and development in addition to more empirical work. The more direct test of modernization theory made here vividly demonstrates the need for new and different theoretical perspectives.

Lasch's point is an excellent one, and if this area of study is going to grow, his challenge must be taken seriously. Part of the problem has been the operating assumption underlying most of the research. Because of the empirical nature of the research, it has been implicitly assumed that a concern for theoretical and ideological conceptions was unnecessary. Almost any recent text on social research will argue quite effectively to the contrary (cf., Phillips, 1976: Chapter 1 and 2). An important step for the future would be, at a minimum, to state what have often been implicit and unexamined assumptions and test them. This would be in stark contrast to much of the previous work, which has concentrated on only methological and technical issues. Several difficulties result from the implicit theoretical approach employed in most of the research. First, it is not always clear or easy to determine which theoretical perspective is being utilized. Lasch clearly believes that modernization theory is the primary perspective being applied in most of the research; but another perspective is plainly implied in much of the work. This perspective could be labeled the stability theory and is most clearly stated by Levy (1965) and would encompass what Lasch (1975a) might call stagnant nucleation theory. Research which illustrates this approach is set on testing and providing evidence for the idea that social order, organization, and relationships have remained virtually constant over time. So at least two different "grand" theoretical perspectives can be identified, and because of this area's interdisciplinary nature (Hareven, 1971), many other theoretical or conceptual approaches can be noted. Hence, it is often a difficult task to determine which perspective (or perspectives) is being employed in a given research project. The implicit nature of these theoretical perspectives also inhibits the development and testing of relevant hypotheses. One has to look long and hard in the literature to find plainly stated and testable hypotheses. Most so-called hypotheses could more appropriately be designated as the focus statement(s) of the study. Finally, without testable hypotheses which are derived from a theory, no means is available by which to empirically confirm or challenge the theory. Thus, it is essential that future quantitative work on a social history of the family go beyond its heretofore narrow focus upon technical and methological issues. Becoming more concerned with theoretical issues should result in the criticism and development that Lasch would like. At a minimum, it should produce better research questions. Finally, what Goode (1964:4) wrote even before most of the work reviewed here was initiated or completed still holds true, which is that "theory without facts is blind speculation; facts without theory are random and often insignificant observations."

The potential for quantification research in the family history area is unlimited. Much work has been done and this discussion speaks to the uses and limitations of this work. Hopefully this discussion will indicate and suggest what the future development of this area should be.

Further Empirical Research Suggested by this Study

As the limitations and gaps of this study are noted, the concerns that require further empirical research become clear. Not only does the work itself pose additional questions, but these limitations and gaps, which are far from unique for work of this kind, suggest other questions that must be dealt with in the future.

A particular area that needs much more attention and research is the role that the family has played as an institution in affecting other social institutions and societal processes. This becomes even more important in light of the apparent historical stability of family structure. If the family has not been as flexible as believed, it must certainly be more than a passive agent in societal change. Very little supportive research is available, but several works have noted the active role of the family in the development of industrialization (cf., Goode, 1963, 1964, 1968; Harris, 1969). In the initial development of industrialization a surplus of capital is a necessary requirement. The family unit is important because prior to industrialization this capital was usually owned and controlled by families or individuals, not companies or organizations. Since the basis for wealth in a preindustrial society is usually land; it is the family-owned and -run farms which must produce the surpluses necessary (usually agricultural products) to amass the necessary capital. In the beginning of American industrialization, the family was frequently the work unit, that is, families, not individuals, were frequently hired or contracted to produce particular products.

Furthermore, the family as the key socializing agent plays a very active role in the development of industrialization. The family performs a vital role by influencing and promoting the beliefs and attitudes that are conducive to industrial development. This influence is not simply limited to the initial years of child rearing. In fact, for individuals actively involved in a family unit, the unit continually provides a set of social forces which either supports or rejects certain types of attitudes and behavior. The family then plays a constant role of reacting either positively or negatively to the attitudes and behavior required by the new systems of production inherent in industrialization [for supporting evidence, see McLaughlin's (Gordon, 1973:136-151) work on Buffalo's Italians]. Hence, the family ultimately decides upon the legitimation of particular values, attitudes, and behavior.

Finally, the family as a unit of reproduction plays an important role in industrial growth. How the family fulfills this function affects the size of the population and the available labor supply. For example, note the growing alarm in the Soviet Union concerning a manpower crunch which is expected within five to ten years. Resulting from sharply lowered birth rates which started in the 1950s, the manpower needs of the job market and armed forces will in the near future outdistance the available supply of youth (Population Reference Bureau, Inc., 1977). Of course, it is the family which supplies the individuals who fill all the society's institutional roles. In addition, fluctuations in the fulfillment of this function (reproduction) causes shifting demands in the types and amounts of goods and services needed from various institutions (e.g., the great need for teachers and school buildings in the 1960s).

Two different approaches have been used in exploring the role of the family during the industrialization and urbanization of a society. One is that many family patterns thought to result from industrialization and urbanization actually were a precondition for many of the economic and technological changes that were a part of industrial growth (Adams, 1975:66). For example, during the American colonial period, the small nuclear family was imported by English settlers (Greenfield, 1967:322), the choice of a spouse was relatively free and was usually based upon love, and there was more equality between the sexes than suggested by the ideal patriarchal pattern (Lantz et al., 1968:413-426). At the end of the colonial period and during the beginning of the national period, additional evidence on the American family has also been reported. Marital strains which reduced family cohesion were apparently present in marriage during this period (Furstenberg, 1966:337), and there was a breakdown in the family's control over marriage, migration, and premarital sexual behavior (Smith, 1973a, 1973b). Since these patterns did not result from the demands of industrialization and urbanization, they were possibly a necessary precondition to their development.

The other related approach would argue that these patterns simply eased the adaptation of the United States in becoming an industrial society. This is a more cross-cultural approach than the previous one and suggests that for preindustrial societies varying states of readiness existed prior to industrial growth. The traditional perspectives of family change implied that all family systems and societies shared roughly the same characteristics prior to industrialization and urbanization. However, several works (cf., Benson, 1971:333-335; Goode, 1963:114-116; 1968) argued that certain characteristics for a society's family system are more conducive to industrial growth. In comparing the industrial growth of Japan to China, Goode (1963-115) argued that the former had several family patterns, lacking in the latter, which facilitated this development. The inheritance system, the feelings of personal loyalty, and the types of occupations given the highest status in Japan made an important contribution to its much more rapid industrialization as compared to China. This is important for the United States as well because several factors were present which contributed to a greater state of readiness. As already mentioned, the family exhibited most of the patterns that industrialization was supposed to bring about prior to its development in the United States. From the beginning, the American environment had some rather unique conditions which aided its industrial growth (see Chapter 4). Beside the physical and climatic advantages, America was a land without established traditions. Hence, the adaptation to a new environment relatively free of kin, who could provide support for the traditional family system, provided a situation for experimentation and the possible change of some family patterns brought from England. This situation was continued even after initial settlement in the colonies as the population experienced a high level of geographical mobility. This trait, which supposedly is only an integral part of industrialized societies, was also very promiment in the nineteenth century. As this study's data indicate, for each census the majority of the population had either immigrated or had migrated within this country. The American environment and the high level of geographical mobility were conducive to an emphasis upon several doctrines, such as individualism, secularism, humanism, and democrary (see Chapter 1) which were supportive of the patterns found in the colonial and early American family. Hence, various factors had already shaped the American family so that its characteristics were primed and ready for industrial development. Thus, it is important to be able to document the family system that existed in a society before industrialization and urbanization. This argument also suggests the possible uniqueness of the American family in its lack of reaction to the processes of industrialization and urbanization. In this sense, the American family may have acted as a catalyst in speeding industrialization and urbanization, but it remained relatively unchanged in this process.

It is essential that the role of the family in social change be reevaluated and that further research be done to document the importance and extent of this role. As one researcher has commented, there has been an increasing amount of evidence presented to suggest that located within the family are "the basic determinants of historical change" (Saveth, 1969:329).

The analysis of the relationship between the processes of industrialization and urbanization and the family indicates that the previous view of family change has been rather limited. In part the family has been less passive than presumed to be the case but some important changes in the structural aspects of the family did occur. The need is not only to try other measures of these two processes but to explore other processes in society that may have played a role in the family changes that did occur. There are several other processes in society, such as the knowledge explosion, the changing belief systems, and the growth in communication, which are not considered completely a part of or resulting from industrialization or urbanization. In other words, this study suggests the usefulness of expanding our explanation of family change beyond the traditional factors that have been emphasized. As B. Laslett (1973:27) noted dealing with similar problems and data, neither demographic nor economic indices can, by themselves, explain household or family organization. Laslett found that historical background and events and political factors played an important part in explaining the various types of family and household organizations that were a part of her sample. An example of this type of factor is offered in this study by the apparent effect of the Civil War (although not anticipated at the outset of this study) upon various family aspects, especially in the South.

A complete understanding of family change is obviously a difficult endeavor. While the data, analysis, and arguments presented here should aid in our understanding of family change, this study has also confirmed the complex nature of this change and of the family's relationship to other processes and institutions. Much challenging work remains to be done.

BIBLIOGRAPHY

ADAMS, B. N. (1975) *The American Family: A Sociological Interpretation.* Chicago: Rand McNally.

ANDERSON, M. (1971) *Family Structure in Nineteenth Century Lancashire.* New York: Cambridge University Press.

ARENSBERG, C. M. (1975) "American communities." *American Anthropologist* 57 (December):1143-1162.

ARIES, P. (1962) *Centuries of Childhood.* New York: Alfred A Knopf.

AXELROD, M. (1956) "Urban structure and social participation." *American Sociological Review* 21 (February):13-18.

AYDELOTTE, W., A. G. BOGUE, and R. W. FOGEL (1972) *The Dimension of Quantitative Research in History.* Princeton, N.J.: Princeton University Press.

BARZUM, J. and H. GRAFF (1957) *The Modern Researcher.* New York: Harcourt, Brace.

BELL, N. W. and E. VOGEL (1960) *A Modern Introduction to the Family.* New York: Free Press.

BENSON, L. (1971) *The Family Bond: Marriage, Love, and Sex in America.* New York: Random House.

BERKNER, L. K. (1972) "The Stem family and the developmental cycle of the peasant household: an 18th century Austrian example." *American Historical Review* 77 (April):398-418.

——— (1975) "The use and misuse of census data for the historical analysis of family structure." *Journal of Interdisciplinary History* 5 (Spring):721-738.

BLALOCK, H. M. (1960) *Social Statistics.* New York: McGraw-Hill.

BLOOMBERG, S. E., M. F. FOX, R. M. WARNER, and S. B. WARNER, Jr. (1971) "A census probe into nineteenth-century family history: southern Michigan, 1850-1880." *Journal of Social History,* 5 (Fall):26-45.

BOALT, G. (1965) *Family and Marriage.* New York: David McKay.

BURCH, T. K. (1967) "The size and structure of families: a comparative analysis of census data." *American Sociological Review* 32 (June):347-363.

BURGESS, E. W. and H. J. LOCKE (1953) *The Family: From Institution to Companionship.* New York: American Book Company.

———— and M. M. THOMES (1963) *The Family: From Institution to Companionship.* New York: American Book Company.

CALHOUN, A. W. (1917-1919) *A Social History of the American Family: From Colonial Times to the Present.* Three Volumes. Cleveland: Arthur H. Clark.

CAMPBELL, R. B. (1974) "Planters and plain folk: Harrison County Texas, as a test case, 1850-1860." *Journal of Southern History* 40 (August):369-398.

COALE, A. and M. ZELNIK (1963) *New Estimates of Fertility and Population in the United States.* Princeton, N.J.: Princeton University Press.

COLLVER, A. (1963) "The family cycle in India and United States." *American Sociological Review* 28 (February):86-96.

CREMIN, L. A. (1974) "The family as educator: some comments on the recent historiography." *Teachers College Record* 76 (December):250-265.

DAVIS, K. (1945) "The world demographic transition." *Annals of the American Academy of Political and Social Science* 237 (January):1-11.

DEMOS, J. (1965) "Notes of life in Plymouth Colony." *William and Mary Quarterly* Third Series, 22 (April):264-286.

———— (1968) "Families in colonial Bristol, Rhode Island: an exercise in historical demography." *William and Mary Quarterly* Third Series, 25 (October):40-57.

DOTSON, F. (1951) "Patterns of voluntary associations among working class families." *American Sociological Review* 16 (October):691-693.

EDWARDS, A. M. (1943) *Sixteenth Census of the United States: 1940 Population, Comparative Occupations Statistics for the United States 1870 to 1940.* Washington, D.C.: United States Government Printing Office.

EDWARDS, J. [ed.] (1969) *The Family & Change.* New York: Alfred A. Knopf.

EVERSLEY, D.E.C. (1966) "Exploitation of Anglican parish registers by aggregative analysis." Pp. 44-95 in E.A. Wrigley (ed.), *An Introduction to English Historical Demography from the Sixteenth to Nineteenth Century.* New York: Basic Books.

FARBER, B. (1973) "Shifting sands: Tucson elite families in 1870." Paper presented at the annual meetings of the Pacific Sociological Association, 1973.

FARLEY, R. and A. T. HERMOLIN (1971) "Family stability: a comparison of trends between blacks and whites." *American Sociological Review* 36 (February):1-17.

FORSTER, R. (1974) "Quantifying history." *Journal of Interdisciplinary History* 5 (Autumn):303-312.

FURSTENBERG, F. F., Jr. (1966) "Industrialization and the American family: a look backward." *American Sociological Review* 31 (June):326-337.

————, T. HERSHBERG, and J. MODELL (1973) "Family structure and ethnicity: an historical and comparative analysis of the black family." Paper presented at the annual meetings of the American Sociological Association, 1973.

GLASS, D. V. (1965) "Introduction." Pp. 1-20 in D. V. Glass and D.E.C. Eversley (eds.), *Population in History: Essays in Historical Demography.* Chicago: Aldine.

GLICK, P. (1957) *American Family: A Volume in the Census Monograph Series.* New York: John Wiley.

———— and R. PARKE, Jr. (1965) "New approaches in studying the life cycle of the family." *Demography* 2 (1965):187-201.

GOODE, W. J. (1963) *World Revolution and Family Patterns.* New York: Free Press.
———— (1964) *The Family.* Englewood Cliffs, N.J.: Prentice-Hall.
———— (1968) "The role of the family in industrialization." Pp. 64-70 in Robert F. Winch Louis Wolf Goodman (eds.), *Selected Studies in Marriage and the Family.* New York: Holt, Rinehart and Winston.
GORDON, M. [ed.] (1973) *The American Family in Socio-Historical Perspective.* New York: St. Martin's.
GREENFIELD, S. M. (1967) "Industrialization and the family in sociological theory." *American Journal of Sociology* 67 (November):312-322.
GREVEN, P. J., Jr. (1966) "Family structure in seventeenth century Andover, Massachusetts." *William and Mary Quarterly* Third Series, 23 (April):234-356.
———— (1967) "Historical demography and colonial America." *William and Mary Quarterly* Third Series, 24 (July):438-454.
———— (1972) "The average size of families and households in the Province of Massachusetts in 1764 and in the United States in 1790: an overview." Pp. 545-560 in Peter Laslett and Richard Wall, *Household and Family in Past Time.* New York: Cambridge University Press.
HABAKKUK, H. J. (1953) "English population in the eighteenth century." *Economic History Review* 6 (December):117-133.
HAREVEN, T. K. (1971) "The history of the family as an interdisciplinary field." *Journal of Interdisciplinary History* 2 (Autumn):399-414.
HARRIS, C. C. (1969) *Family: An Introduction.* New York: Frederick A. Praeger.
HENRETTA, J. A. (1971) "The morphology of New England society in the colonial period." *Journal of Interdisciplinary History* 2 (Autumn):379-398.
HENRY, L. (1968) "Historical demography." *Daedalus* 97 (Spring):385-396.
HERSHBERG, T. (1973) "A method for the computerized study of family and household structure using the manuscript schedule of the U.S. Census of Population, 1850-1880." *The Family Historical Perspective* 1 (Spring):6-20.
HIGGS, R. and H. L. STETTLER III (1970) "Colonial New England demography: a sampling approach." *William and Mary Quarterly* Third Series, 27 (April):282-293.
HOLLINGSWOTH, T. H. (1969) *Historical Demography.* Ithaca, N.Y.: Cornell University Press.
HORTON, P. B. and C. L. HUNT (1968) *Sociology.* New York: McGraw-Hill.
HSU, F.L.K. (1943) "The myth of Chinese family size." *American Journal of Sociology* 48 (March):555-562.
HUNT, M. (1971) "The future of marriage." *Playboy* 18 (August):116-118, 168-175.
JAHER, F. C. (1970) "Short review of 'nineteenth-century cities: essays in the new urban history'." Thernstrom and Sennett (eds.), *Journal of Interdisciplinary History* 1 (Autumn):195-198.
KEPHART, W. (1961) *The Family, Society, and the Individual.* Boston: Houghton Mifflin.
KLINGAMAN, D. (1971) "Food surpluses and deficits in the American colonies, 1768-1772." *Journal of Economic History* 31 (September):553-569.
KRAUSE, J. T. (1958) "Some implications of recent work in historical demography." *Comparative Studies in Society and History* 1 (October):164-188.
LANG, O. (1946) *Chinese Family and Society.* New Haven: Yale University Press.
LANTZ, H. R. and E. K. ALIX (1970) "Occupational mobility in a nineteenth century Mississippi Valley river community." *Social Science Quarterly* (September):404-408.

LANTZ, H. R., R. SCHMITT, M. BRITTON, and E. SNYDER (1968) "Pre-industrial patterns in the colonial family in America." *American Sociological Review* 33 (June): 413-426.

LANTZ, H. R., J. KEYES, and M. SCHULTZ (1975) "The family in the preindustrial period: from base lines in history to change." *American Sociological Review* 40 (February):21-36.

LANTZ, H. R., R. SCHMITT and R. HERMAN (1973) "The preindustrial family in America: a further examination of early magazines." *American Journal of Sociology* 79 (November):566-588.

LANTZ, H. R., M. SCHULTZ, and M. O'HARA (1977) "The changing American family from preindustrial to the industrial period: a final report." *American Sociological Review* 42 (June):406-421.

LANTZ, H. R. and E. SNYDER (1969) *Marriage: An Examination of the Man-Woman Relationship.* New York: John Wiley.

LASCH, C. (1975a) "The family and history." *New York Review of Books* 22 (November, 13):33-38.

——— (1975b) "The emotions of the family." *New York Review of Books* 22 (November, 27):37-42.

——— (1975c) "What the doctor ordered." *New York Review of Books* 22 (December, 11):50-53.

LASLETT, B. (1973) "Variation in household structure: Los Angeles, California in 1850." Paper presented at the annual meetings of American Sociological Association, August 1973.

LASLETT, P. (1965a) "The history of population and social structure." *International Social Science Journal* 27 (August):582-594.

——— (1965b) *The World We Lost.* New York: Scribner's.

——— (1969) "Size and structure of the household in England over three centuries." *Population Studies* 23 (July):199-224.

——— (1970) "The comparative history of household and family." *Journal of Social History* 4 (Fall):75-87.

——— and J. HARRISON (1963) "Clayworth and Cogenhoe." Pp. 157-184 in H.E. Bell and R.L. Ollard (eds.), *Historical Essays 1600-1750: Presented to David Ogg.* London: Adam and Charles Black.

LASLETT, P. and R. WALL (1972) *Household and Family in Past Time.* New York: Cambridge University Press.

LATHROP, B. (1968) "History from the census returns." in S. M. Lipset and R. Hofstader (eds.), *Sociology and History: Methods.* New York: Basic Books.

LEVY, M. J., Jr. (1949) *The Family Revolution in Modern China.* Cambridge, Mass.: Harvard University Press.

——— (1965) "Aspects of the analysis of family structure." Pp. 40-63 in Ansleys J. Coale et al., *Aspects of the Analysis of Family Structure.* Princeton, N.J.: Princeton University Press.

LITWAK, E. (1960) "Geographic mobility and extended family cohesion." *American Sociological Review* 25 (June):383-395.

LOCKRIDGE, K. A. (1966) "The population of Dedham, Massachusetts, 1636-1736." *Economic History Review* Second Series, 19 (August):318-344.

MARTINSON, F. M. (1970) *Family in Society.* New York: Dodd, Mead.

McKEE, J. B. (1969) *Introduction to Sociology.* New York: Holt, Rinehart and Winston.

McKEOWN, T. and R. G. BROWN (1955) "Medical evidence related to English population change in the eighteenth century." *Population Studies* 9 (November):119-141.

McKEOWN, T. and R. G. RECORD (1962) "Reasons for the decline of mortality in England and Wales during the nineteenth century." *Population Studies* 19 (November):94-122.

MILLER, B. C. (1972) "A computerized method of determining family structure from mid-nineteenth century census data." Unpublished M.S. thesis, University of Pennsylvania, Philadelphia, 1972.

MILLER, D. C. (1970) *Handbook of Research Design and Social Measurement.* New York: David McKay.

MILLS, C. W. (1959) *The Sociological Imagination.* New York: Oxford University Press.

MOLLER, H. (1945) "Sex composition and correlated culture patterns of colonial America." *William and Mary Quarterly* Third Series, 2 (April):113-129.

MURDOCK, G. P. (1949) *Social Structure.* New York: Free Press.

NIE, N. D., H. BENT, and C. H. HULL (1970) *Statistical Package for the Social Sciences.* New York: McGraw-Hill.

NIMKOFF, M. F. (1947) *Marriage and Family,* New York: Houghton Mifflin.

——— (1965) *Comparative Family Systems.* New York: Houghton Mifflin.

NORTON, S. L. (1971) "Population growth in colonial America: a study of Ipswich, Massachusetts." *Population Studies* 25 (November):433-452.

OGBURN, W. F. (1969) "The changing family functions." Pp. 58-63 in R. F. Winch et al. (eds.), *Selected Studies in Marriage and the Family.* New York: Holt, Rinehart and Winston.

——— and M. F. NIMKOFF (1955) *Technology and the Changing Family.* Boston: Houghton Mifflin.

ORENSTEIN, H. (1961) "The recent history of the extended family in India." *Social Problems* 8 (Spring):341-350.

PARKE, R., Jr. (1969) "Changes in household and family structure in the USA." Paper presented at the general conference of the International Union for the Scientific Study of Population, September 1969.

PARSONS, T. (1954) "The kinship system of the contemporary United States." Pp. 177-198 in Talcott Parsons, *Essays in Sociological Theory.* Glencoe, Ill.: Free Press.

——— (1964) *The Social System.* New York: Free Press.

——— (1965) "The normal American family." Pp. 34-36 in S. M. Farber (ed.), *Man and Civilization: The Family's Search for Survival.* New York: McGraw-Hill.

——— and R. BALES (1955) *Family, Socialization, and Interaction Process.* Glencoe, Ill.: Free Press.

PETERSEN, W. (1960) "The demographic transition in The Netherlands." *American Sociological Review* 25 (June):334-347.

——— (1969) *Population.* New York: Macmillan.

PHILLIPS, B. S. (1976) *Social Research: Strategy and Tactics.* New York: Macmillan.

Population Reference Bureau, Inc. (1977) "U.S.S.R. heads for demographic crunch." *Intercom* 5 (September):1, 11.

POTTER, J. (1965) "The growth of population in America, 1700-1860." Pp. 631-688 in D. V. Glass and D. E. C. Eversley (eds.), *Population in History.* Chicago: Aldine.

PRYOR, E. T. (1967) "Rhode Island family structure: 1875 and 1960." Paper presented at annual meetings of Population Association of America, April 1967.

QUEEN, S. A. and D. B. CARPENTAR (1953) *The American City.* New York: McGraw-Hill.

Rand Corporation (1955) "A million random digits with 100,000 normal deviates."
    Glencoe, Ill.: Free Press.
ROSTOW, W. W. (1960) *The Stages of Economic Growth: A Non-Communist Mani-
    festo.* Cambridge, Mass.: Harvard University Press.
SAVETH, E. N. (1969) "The problem of American family history." *American Quarterly*
    21 (Summer):311-329.
SCHNEIDER, E. V. (1957) *Industrial Society.* New York, McGraw-Hill.
SEWARD, R. R. (1973) "The colonial family in America: toward a socio-historical
    restoration of its structure." *Journal of Marriage and the Family* 34 (February):58-70.
——— (1974) "Family size in the United States: an exploratory study of trends." *Kansas
    Journal of Sociology* 10 (Fall):119-136.
——— (1976) "The family versus industrialization and urbanization: occupational roles
    as a potential link." Paper presented at the annual meeting of the Midwest Socio-
    logical Society, April, 1976.
——— (1977) "Household versus family membership in the United States: historic
    trends." Paper presented at the annual meeting of the American Sociological Associa-
    tion, September 1977.
SHORTER, E. (1975) *The Making of the Modern Family.* New York: Basic Books.
SJOBERG, G. (1960) *The Pre-industrial City: Past and Present.* New York: Free Press.
SMITH, D. S. (1972) "The demographic history of Colonial New England." *Journal of
    Economic History* 32 (March):165-184.
——— (1973a) "Parental power and marriage patterns: an analysis of historical trends in
    Hingham, Massachusetts." *Journal of Marriage and the Family* 25 (August):419-428.
——— (1973b) "Changes in American family structure before the demographic transition:
    the case of Hingham, Massachusetts." Presented at the annual meeting of the Society
    for the Study of Social Problems, August 1973.
SPIRO, M. E. (1954) "Is the family universal?" *American Anthropologist* 56 (October):
    839-846.
SPREITZER, E. A. and L. E. RILEY (1970) "Another look at the relationship between
    sociology and history." Paper presented at annual meeting of American Sociological
    Association, Washington, D.C., September 1970.
STEDMAN JONES, G. (1976) "From historical sociology to theoretic history." *British
    Journal of Sociology* 27 (September):295-305.
STONE, L. (1967) *The Crisis of the Aristocracy, 1558-1641.* New York: Oxford University
    Press.
SUSSMAN, M. (1959) "The isolated family: fact or fiction? *Social Problems 6* (Spring):
    333-340.
SUSSMAN, M. B. and L. BURCHINAL (1964) "Kin, family network: unheralded struc-
    ture in current conceptualizations of family functioning." *Marriage and Family Living*
    24 (August):231-240.
TAEUBER, C. and I. B. TAEUBER (1958) *The Changing Population of the United
    States: A Volume in the Census Monograph Series.* New York: John Wiley.
THERNSTROM, S. (1964) *Poverty and Progress: Social Mobility in a Nineteenth
    Century City.* Cambridge, Massachusetts: Harvard University.
——— (1968) "Urbanization, migration, and social mobility in late nineteenth century
    America." Pp. 158-175 in Barton Bernstein (ed.), *Toward a New Past.* New York:
    Pantheon.
United States: Bureau of the Census (1853) *Population of the United States in 1850: The
    Seventh Census.* Volume 1. Washington, D.C.: United States Government Printing
    Office.

———— (1864) *Population of the United States in 1860: The Eighth Census*. Volume 1. Washington, D.C.: United States Government Printing Office.

———— (1866) *Statistics of the United States in 1860: The Eighth Census*. Volume 4. Washington, D.C.: United States Government Printing Office.

———— (1872a) *Ninth Census*. Volume 1. The Statistics of the Population of the United States. Washington, D.C.: United States Government Printing Office.

———— (1872b) *Ninth Census*. Volume 3. The Statistics of the Wealth and Industry of the United States. Washington, D.C.: United States Government Printing Office.

———— (1872c) *Ninth Census of the United States: Statistics of the Population*. Tables I-VIII Inclusive. Washington, D.C.: United States Government Printing Office.

———— (1883a) *Statistics of the Population of the United States at Tenth Census*. Volume 1, Washington, D.C.: United States Government Printing Office.

———— (1883b) *Report of the Manufactures of the United States at the Tenth Census*. Washington, D.C.: United States Government Printing Office.

———— (1933) *Population Bulletin: Families — United States Summary*. Washington, D.C.: United States Government Printing Office.

———— (1943) *Sixteenth Census of the United States: 1940 Population. Comparative Occupation Statistics for the United States, 1870 to 1940*. Washington, D.C.: United States Government Printing Office.

———— (1944) *Population: Families-Size of Family and Age of Head*. Washington, D.C.: United States Government Printing Office.

———— (1949) *Historical Statistics of the United States: 1789-1945*. Washington, D.C.: United States Government Printing Office.

———— (1953a) *Census of Housing: 1950*. Volume 1. General Characteristics. Part 1. U.S. Summary. Washington, D.C.: United States Government Printing Office.

———— (1953b) *U.S. Census of Population: 1950*. Volume 2. Characteristics of the Population. Part 1. U.S. Summary. Washington, D.C.: United States Government Printing Office.

———— (1955) *U.S. Census of Population: 1950*. Volume 4. Special Reports. Part 2, Chapter A, General Characteristics of Families. Washington, D.C.: United States Government Printing Office.

———— (1960a) *Historical Statistics of the United States: Colonial Times to 1957*. Washington, D.C.: United States Government Printing Office.

———— (1960b) *1960 Census of Population: Classified Index of Occupations and Industries*. Washington, D.C.: United States Government Printing Office.

———— (1961) *United States Census of Population: 1960*. Volume 1. Characteristics of the Population: Part A. Number of Inhabitants. Washington, D.C.: United States Government Printing Office.

———— (1963a) *United States Census of Population: 1960*. Subject Report Families. Final Report. Pc(2) - 4A. Washington, D.C.: United States Government Printing Office.

———— (1963b) *United States Census of Population: 1960*. Volume 1. Detailed Characteristics. U.S. Summary. Final Report. PC (1) - 20. Washington, D.C.: United States Government Printing Office.

———— (1964) *United States Census of Population: 1960*. Volume 1. Characteristics of Population. Part 1. U.S. Summary. Washington, D.C.: United States Government Printing Office.

———— (1965) *Historical Statistics of the United States: Colonial Times to 1957 (Continuation to 1962 and Revisions)*. Washington, D.C.: United States Government Printing Office.

———— (1973a) *Census of Population: 1970.* Subject Reports. Final Report. PC (2) - 4A. Family Composition. Washington, D.C.: United States Government Printing Office.

———— (1973b) *Census of Population: 1970.* Subject Reports. Final Report. PC (2) - 4D. Age at First Marriage. Washington, D.C: United States Government Printing Office.

VINOVSKIS, M. A. (1971) "The 1789 life table of Edward Wigglesworth." *Journal of Economic History* 31 (September):570-590.

———— (1972) "Mortality rates and trends in Massachusetts before 1860." *Journal of Economic History* 32 (March):184-213.

WEBER, M. (1958) *The Protestant Ethic and the Spirit of Capitalism.* New York: Scribner's.

WELLS, R. B. (1971) "Family size and fertility control in eighteenth-century America: a study of Quaker families." *Population Studies* 25 (March):73-82.

WERTENBAKER, T. J. (1929) *The First Americans, 1607-1690.* New York: Macmillan.

WILENSKY, H. and C. LEBEAUX (1958) *Industrial Society and Social Welfare.* New York: Russell Sage.

WIRTH, L. (1938) "Urbanism as a way of life." *American Journal of Sociology* 44 (July): 1-24.

WOZNIAK, P. R. (1972) "Family systems, industrialization and demographic factors: an appraisal of the arguments and evidence." Paper presented at the annual meeting of the American Sociological Association, August 1972.

WRIGHT, C. D. (1900) *The History and Growth of the United States Census.* Washington, D.C.: United States Government Printing Office.

WRIGLEY, E. A. (1966a) "Family limitation in pre-industrial England." *Economic History Review* Second Series, 19 (April):82-109.

———— (1966b) "Family Reconstitution." Pp. 96-159 in E. A. Wrigley (ed.), *An introduction to English Historical Demography from the Sixteenth to Nineteenth Century.* New York: Basic Books.

MICROFILM

United States: Bureau of the Census (1971) *Seventh Census Population Schedules.* Microfilm Publication Number 432. Rolls 30, 31, 67, 75, 182, 184, 230, 233, 264-267, 332-339, 350, 354, 393, 404, 505, 517-522, 749, 835, 909, and 916.

———— *Eighth Census Population Schedules.* Microfilm Publication Number M653. Rolls 50, 52, 119, 129, 311, 322, 409, 413, 445-447, 443, 518-526, 544, 549, 610, 629, 754, 763-776, 1069, 1070, 1193, 1194, 1289, and 1307.

———— *Ninth Census Population Schedules.* Microfilm Publication Number M593. Rolls 63, 66, 146, 160, 376, 391, 508, 517, 552-556, 638-650, 671, 684, 763, 787, 937, 946-963, 1300-1301, 1464, 1578, and 1607.

———— *Tenth Census Population Schedules.* Microfilm Publication Number T9. Rolls 56, 58-59, 143, 154, 326-327, 339-340, 449, 456-457, 485-487, 549-562, 579, 589, 676-677, 699, 833-834, 840-857, 1095-1096, 1202-1203, 1294, and 1330. Washington, D.C.: National Archives and Records Service.

APPENDIX A:
Definitions of Variables

Family Variables

Family of residence—At least two persons related by blood, marriage, or adoption who reside in the same dwelling place.

Primary family—The family of residence which contains the head of the household.

Primary family household—When primary family membership is equal to its household membership.

Secondary families—Any additional families of residence, such as lodgers or resident employees, which do not contain any members of the primary family.

Family size—All members of the family of residence.

Nuclear family—Any family of residence which is composed of a married couple with or without children, or one parent with one or more child.

Horizontally extended families—A family of residence consisting of one or more generations with two or more marital pairs occurring in one of the generations.

Vertically extended families—A family of residence consisting of three or more generations.

Number of generations—Counting each stage of descent within the family of residence.

Subfamily—A nuclear family which is related to, but not including, the head of the household or his spouse.

Number of marital pairs—All married couples present within the family of residence.

Number of children—All offspring of the family head's nuclear family residing in the family of residence.

Primary individual—The head of a household who either lives alone or with one or more nonrelatives.

Nonrelatives—Any person not related to the household head including lodgers and/or resident employees.

Age of wife—Reported age for head of family's wife or female family head.

Industrialization Variables

Period of industrialization—The history of the United States is divided into three periods of industrial growth—preindustrial, industrialization, and postindustrial.

Occupational group—Classifying the family head's occupation into one of nine categories based upon Edwards' (1943) occupation scale developed for the U.S. Bureau of the Census.

Occupational substitutability—Classifying the family head's occupational group according to its amount of specialization and differentiation as discussed by Harris (1969).

Nonextractive occupations in state—Percentage of persons employed in a sample state's industries other than agriculture, fishing, mining, forestry, and logging.

Mining occupations in state—Percentage of persons employed in the mining industry for a sample state's industries.

County's employees engaged in manufacturing—Percentage of county's potential labor force (25% of population) employed in manufacturing establishments.

Geographical mobility—When place of birth is different than residence at time of census for head of family of residence

Urbanization Variables

Population density of county—Population divided by number of square miles in the county.

Population growth of country—Percentage of increase over previous census relative to population size of county at previous census.

Percentage of county's population in census designated areas—Urban:

Place with 2,500 inhabitants or more that is an incorporated city, borough, or village. Nonurban incorporated area: Population living in incorporated areas with less than 2,500 inhabitants. Rural: All persons living outside of incorporated areas.

Location of family's household—Whether located in urban, nonurban community, rural nonfarm, or rural farm area.

Other Variables

Time—The decade from which the sample unit is taken.

Real estate value—The value listed for property owned by the family head.

APPENDIX B:
Sampling Procedure

The selection, collection, and preparation of data for the nineteenth century sample of households was supported in part by a grant, GS-33863, from the National Science Foundation.

Individual selection of families from all the available individual manuscript census schedules for the U.S. population from 1850 to 1880 would be too expensive and nearly impossible. To facilitate the selection of a sample and, at the same time, provide a representative sample, a stratified cluster sampling procedure was used. The states (29) that were part of the United States as of January 1850 constituted the geographical boundaries of the area from which the sample of households was drawn. As a result, the greater part of the area covered lies east of the Mississippi River. The only states west of the Mississippi were Arkansas, Iowa, Louisiana, and Texas (which, by chance, were all used in the sample).

Territorial areas as of 1850 and the District of Columbia were eliminated from the sampling process. The territorial areas were excluded for several reasons. First, they lacked the county units or equivalent civil divisions necessary to the application of the sampling procedure. Second, the territories were very sparsely populated, and the population that did exist was usually concentrated in one or more relatively small geographical areas within the territory. This fact, added to the extreme mobility of the population, made the territories difficult to enumerate. In some cases, the same type of data was not collected or was not as easily collected as in the states. For the District of Columbia the lack of counties or equivalents was again a decisive factor. The fact that the District's population was an artifical collection provided additional support for not attempting to overcome the difficulties of the first reason.

The first step in the sampling procedure was to place all of the states (29) into one of three strata—Northeast, North Central (Mid-west), and South. The Northeast stratum consisted of Connecticut, Maine, Massachusetts, New Hampshire, New Jersey, New York, Pennsylvania, Rhode Island, and Vermont. The North Central stratum consisted of Illinois, Indiana, Iowa, Michigan, Missouri, Ohio, and Wisconsin. The South stratum consisted of Alabama, Arkansas, Delaware, Florida, Georgia, Kentucky, Louisiana, Maryland, Mississippi, North Carolina, South Carolina, Tennessee, Texas, Virginia and, starting with the 1870 census, West Virginia.

A number of considerations led to this stratification. First, the state strata represent different geographical regions in the United States. Also, to allow comparisons to data from later censuses, the state strata were based upon the same regional divisions used by the United States Census Bureau (1960a: xii, 16, 18, 20, 25) during the twentieth century. Furthermore, the state strata are domains of the study indicating that separate data from each stratum should yield additional information. This is possible because of differences in population, population growth, and economies between the strata. In the 1850 census, the South strata led slightly in population with the Northeast stratum second. The North Central stratum was the least populated. Over the years sampled, the population of the North Central region increased at the highest rate with the Northeast second. The South exhibited the lowest rate of growth. Throughout the sample period, the economy of the Northeast stratum relied most heavily upon mining and the manufacture of goods while the South's economy relied prodominantly upon its agricultural products. The biggest change occurred in the North Central stratum which in 1850 relied heavily upon agricultural and lumber products. As time progressed, its economy became more like the Northeast stratum. These distinctions between the strata suggest a type of homegeneity within each stratum. A comparison between strata should provide additional information relevant to the concern with the industrialization process. This is based upon the existence of differential rates of industrialization for the strata.

With each stratum a cluster of four states was selected through the use of a random number table. Rand's (1955) book of random numbers and its suggested procedure was used. Before selection each state was weighted according to the size of its population within the strata. This weighting procedure assured that people in the less populated states within each stratum would not be overrepresented in the cluster of the four states selected.

After the twelve states or the primary sampling units were selected the next step was to select the secondary sampling units which were smaller civil divisions within each selected state. The units used were counties or the equivalent. From each state two counties were selected. Before selection, all counties in each state chosen were stratified into two strata based upon the population of the counties. From each state one county was selected from the stratum containing the most populated counties and one county was selected from the stratum of lesser populated counties. To determine in which stratum of counties a county was located, its position in relation to the median size of counties for that particular state was used. Those counties above the median were in one stratum and those below in the other stratum. With the strata determined, each county was weighted according to its population size and one county was selected randomly (using the same procedure used for the selection of states) from each stratum.

After the secondary sampling units (twenty-four counties) were selected, the final step was to obtain the family units or primary selections. Using a systematic sampling procedure—after a random start of selecting every unit at a predetermined and fixed interval—one hundred dwelling units were chosen from each of the twenty-four counties. Then, in each of the selected sample dwelling units, the family unit or units were determined and measured for the structural aspects of the family and other characteristics being studied.

The use of counties within regions provides an additional advantage. The extent to which regions vary depends to a large extent upon where their boundaries are drawn. No matter how regions are defined they "merge into one another; but for statistical analysis the line must be sharp" (Peterson, 1969:106). Despite this problem and because of practical considerations, the boundaries used to determine the sample strata correspond to the administrative units used by the census, i.e., states and counties. A very practical consideration in selecting county units was the the microfilm on which the original manuscript census schedules were recorded are organized by counties within each state. For most of the smaller counties their complete set of census schedules are available on one microfilm roll. The use of counties offered a great savings in time and cost. In addition, each county is much more homogeneous in its economic and social characteristics than are regions and states. This is particularly useful for an analysis of the process of industrialization and urbanization.

APPENDIX C:

Recounting Procedure for Household and Family Structures from U.S. Census Original Manuscript Schedules (1850-1880)

The following is a summary statement concerning the guidelines and procedures applied to determine the composition of the study's sample households which were located on census manuscript schedules. For definitions of terms used below, see Appendix A.)

Although the data are not entirely complete except for one census or completely accurate, a great deal of information is available to help determine (infer) each member's position within a household. Beginning with the 1850 census, each individual inhabitant of a household was listed by name (usually including first as well as family name) plus other additional information about the individual. The information used was name, age, sex, position in household listing, and birth place. The values for these characteristics of each individual determined his or her family and/or household position. The pivotal position was household head in that all other positions were discerned and/or described by their relationship to the head. The only exception was for the 1880 census manuscript schedules which, in addition to the above information, reported the relationship of each household member to the head. It was only for the 1850, 1860, and 1870 censuses that the relationships had to be inferred. The 1880 schedules were used to develop the recounting procedure applied to the earlier censuses and to estimate the amount of error that occurred in the recount. In addition, the experience gained from an earlier exploration study (Seward, 1974) was utilized in developing the recounting procedure.

The first step performed for each sample household unit was to determine the membership of the primary family and the membership of any existing secondary families and to eliminate any nonrelatives present who were resident employees or lodgers. Two criteria were used to determine this breakdown. First, family or common surname was considered an indication of membership in the same family. Since the most typical family unit was nuclear in structure, the majority of households were made up of individuals all sharing the same surname—a primary family.

Sole reliance upon sharing a common family name would eliminate some relatives who had a different surname, however, To minimize this problem, the order in which individuals were presented was taken into consideration. The instructions given to the census marshals in 1850 with regard to the order of the listing individuals in each household were the following:

> The names were to be written beginning with father and mother; or if either or both be dead, begin with some other ostensible head of family; to be followed, as far as practicable with the names of the oldest child residing at home, then the next oldest, and so on to the youngest, then the inmates, lodgers and servants (Wright, 1900: 151).

Instructions for the later censuses lack any further detail. Wright (1900) also provides a more inclusive order by which the household members were usually listed. This list is as follows: household head, spouse, unmarried children of head, married children of head, grandchildren, parents and parents-in-law, other relatives, servants, boarders, etc. Previous experience and the 1880 data suggest that the household members were presented in this order by far the greatest part of the time. Another recent work dealing with the same census material also confirmed this order (Miller, 1972:27-28). One of the most common exceptions was for parents of the head or spouse who sometimes had a different surname to be listed before the children. (Miller [1972] also noted this exception.)

Together these criteria were used to determine family membership. Again, initial divisions were made on the basis of common surname. Any individuals having surnames different from the family head's but listed in a position indicating family membership and having the appropriate age or sex characteristics were included as family members, e.g., a male, female, or couple following the spouse or a male household head. If these individuals had a different surname from that of the head but ages suggesting that they might be parents of the head's spouse and/ or were followed by a number of children having a similar surname as that of the head, they were included as family members.

Toward the end of the listing order, the separation of other relatives from resident employees or lodgers was most difficult. In this area of the order common surname was the determining criterion with very few exceptions. Initially, children included in the list of offspring having a different surname were separated out of family units in order to get a more accurate count of the head's wife or female head's own children for the particular marriage at the time of the census. However, those children who were in positions (in the chronological list of children) suggesting step-children* of either parent were remerged with the appropriate primary family when determining other family aspects. Also the larger the family, the easier the task of determining relationships because there were more positions listed.

Once family membership was established, the next step was to determine a number of structural aspects for the family. To do this, the relationship within the family had to be established. This was done using the following four variables: age, sex, position in listing, and, less frequently, birth place. The listing order expected for the family members was the first criterion used to determine the relationships within the family. Then sex and age characteristics were used to confirm these relationships. Birth place was sometimes used to provide further evidence of sibling relationships. The person listed first in the household with a primary family or first in a secondary family was considered the family head. The family head was the pivotal position in determining family positions. Table C.1 gives the typical types of relationships found in the sample and the rules used to establish them for the 1850, 1860 and 1870 sample census data.

These rules were adequate to cover most situations and relationships. However, a limited number of cases arose in which the procedure either did not apply or the information was inadequate. In these cases individual decisions were made based upon what information was available, past experience, and what seemed to be appropriate. The chance of error in inferring family relationships also increase as one proceeds down the list of relationships. Miller (1972:33) found the same difficulty in his much more sophisticated study that developed procedures to determine family relationships for the 1850 to 1870 censuses.

For any secondary family units (not containing the household head), determined when dividing household members into family units, the

---

*It is assumed that adopted children would have the same surname.

Table C.1: Characteristics Used to Determine Family Relationships for 1850, 1860, and 1870 (from Census Manuscript Schedules)

Relationship	Location	Sex	Name	Age
Wife	Follows male head of family	F	Same	She and head must be at least 16 years old. Not more than 30 years younger than head. If much younger than head, must be at least 5 years older than oldest child.
Husband	Follows female head of family	M	Same	He and head must be at least 16 years old. Husband usually older than head. Not more than 16 years older than head.
Child	Follows the head, head's spouse, another older child, married child and family, family head's sibling, sibling's family, or parent or parent-in-law of head.	M or F	Same	Son or daughter are at least 16 years younger than head.
Step-Child	Same as above	M or F	Different	Son or daughter are at least 16 years younger than head.
Married Child	Same as above	M or F	Either same or different	Married child is at least 16 years younger than head.
Grandchild	Same as above	M or F	Either	Grandchild is at least 16 years younger than previously mentioned married child and/or at least 32 years younger than head.
Parent	Same as above	M or F	Either	Parent is at least 16 years older than head or spouse depending on which is considered to be their child.
Brother	Same as above	M or F	Either	Siblings must be either less than 16 years younger or no more than 16 years older than head or spouse depending on which is considered to be blood relative. If surnames different, place of birth was criterion.

Table C.1 (Continued):

Relationship	Location	Sex	Name	Age	
Subfamily head	Same as above	M or F	Either		Head of any nuclear family unit in the family that does not include the family head. The relationships for subfamily members were determined applying the above rules.
Other	Same as above	M or F	Either		Any individual because of his or her name, age, sex, or position who is a family member but does not fit into any of above categories. Surname was the primary criterion used here.

same rules as presented above were applied to establish family relationships.

Finally, those individuals not considered members of either a primary or secondary family unit were classified as either resident employees or lodgers. The criterion was that individuals with an occupation listed were resident employees and those without were lodgers.

Although the rules were valid in most cases, all possible situations could not be considered prior to the recount. In fact, several situations defy categorization due to such variables as the individuals doing the recording (use of instructions, handwriting, etc.), the individual providing the information, and so forth. Hence, allowances had to be made for these individual differences and unique decisions had to be made based upon the available evidence.

APPENDIX D:
Occupation Code

A list of the occupations frequently reported on the 1850 to 1880 original census manuscript schedules was made and code numbers were assigned to each of these occupations. The code numbers assigned were based upon a scheme developed by Alba Edwards (1943) and a similar but more current census classification of occupation groups (Miller, 1970:172-173). The occupation for each head of a family and/or household which was reported and readable was classified into one of the following groups which had a corresponding range of numbers:

Occupational Group	Code Number Range
Professional and technical workers	10-19
Business managers, officials and proprietors	20-29
Clerical workers	30-39
Craftman and foreman	40-49
Operatives	50-59
Private household workers	60-69
Service workers, except private household	70-79
Unskilled laborers including farmer	80-89
Unclassified occupations	90-97
	98

Within each group a number of the more common occupations were given specific numbers, for example in the professional group, clergyman was code 10. But the majority of the occupations were classified in the "other" category and given the highest number possible within a given occupational group's range. For example, if a particular occupation was considered a professional one but had no specific assigned code it was given the code number 19.

The attempt was made to classify these nineteenth century occupations into groups that would be comparable to the groups used in contemporary census data. In addition, assigning some of the more common occupations unique numbers meant that further analysis could be performed for certain specific occupations. Finally, the occupations listed do not include every occupation found on the census schedules as inclusion was based upon state summary lists and/or being reported several times on the schedules. For those occupations with no code, an individual decision was made to either place the occupation in an "other" category of an occupational group or code it as unclassifiable.

The complete list of occupations and their corresponding codes is available from the author upon request.

ABOUT THE AUTHOR

RUDY RAY SEWARD is an Assistant Professor in the Department of Sociology and Anthropology, North Texas State University. He holds a Ph.D. in sociology from Southern Illinois University, Carbondale. A recipient of several research fellowships and grants, Dr. Seward was the winner of the National Council on Family Relations 1972 Student Award in Family Studies. His areas of interest include family, urbanization, industrialization, and social change. Among his recent publications are "American Schools of Sociologists" (with Gunnar Boalt and Helena Herlin) in Boalt et al. (eds.), *Communication and Communication Barriers in Sociology* (Uppsala, Sweden: Almquist och Wiksell, 1976); and "The Colonial Family in America: Toward a Socio-Historical Restoration of Its Structure," in Dyer (ed.) *The American Family: Variety and Change* (New York: McGraw-Hill, 1978).